THE VISUAL
DICTIONARY *of the*
EARTH

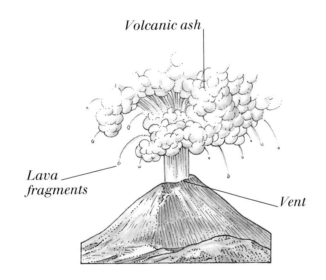

Volcanic ash

Lava fragments

Vent

ACTIVE VOLCANO

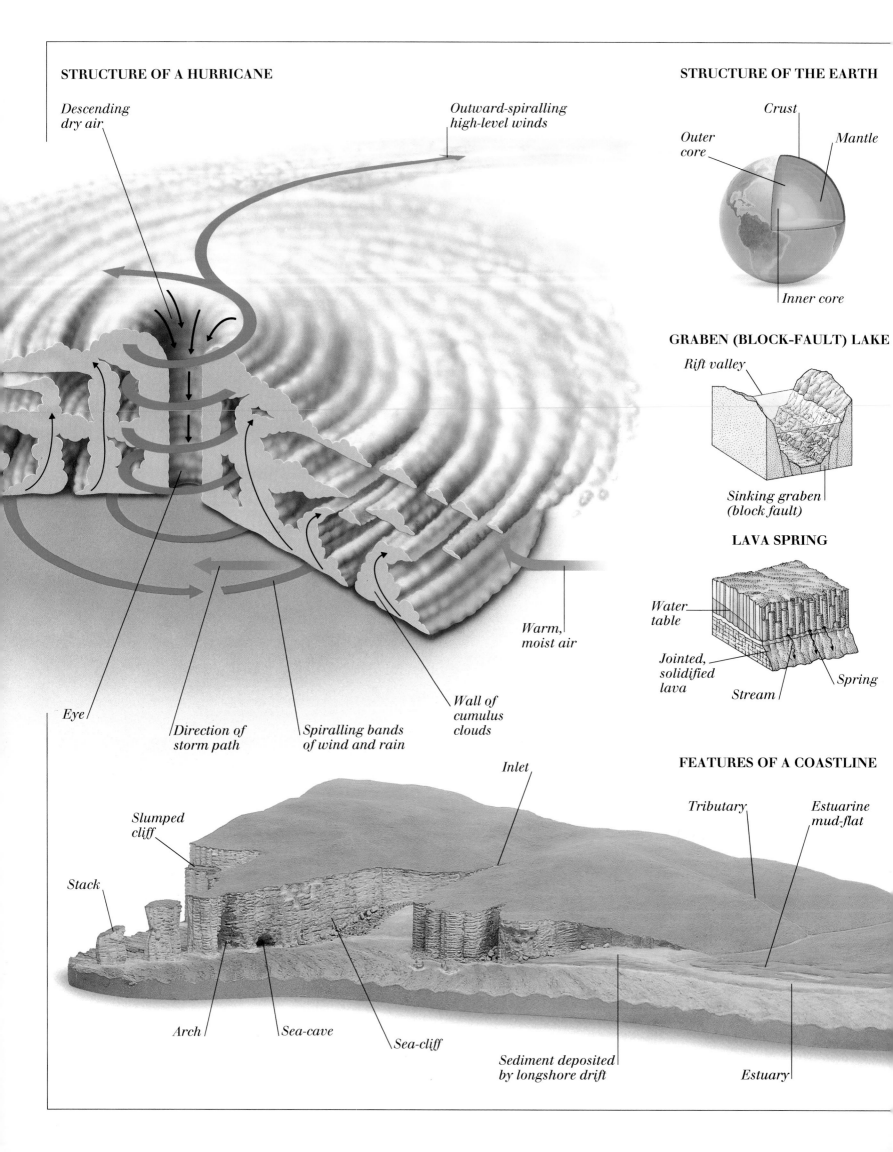

STRUCTURE OF A HURRICANE

Descending dry air

Outward-spiralling high-level winds

Eye

Direction of storm path

Spiralling bands of wind and rain

Wall of cumulus clouds

Warm, moist air

STRUCTURE OF THE EARTH

Crust

Outer core

Mantle

Inner core

GRABEN (BLOCK-FAULT) LAKE

Rift valley

Sinking graben (block fault)

LAVA SPRING

Water table

Jointed, solidified lava

Stream

Spring

FEATURES OF A COASTLINE

Inlet

Tributary

Estuarine mud-flat

Slumped cliff

Stack

Arch

Sea-cave

Sea-cliff

Sediment deposited by longshore drift

Estuary

THE VISUAL
DICTIONARY *of the*
EARTH

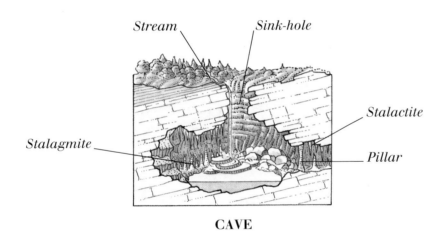

Stream

Sink-hole

Stalactite

Stalagmite

Pillar

CAVE

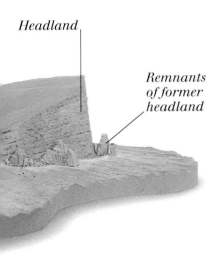

Headland

Remnants
*of former
headland*

COVENT
GARDEN
BOOKS

A DORLING KINDERSLEY BOOK

PROJECT ART EDITOR JOHNNY PAU
DESIGNER PAUL CALVER

PROJECT EDITOR GEOFFREY STALKER
CONSULTANT EDITOR MARTYN BRAMWELL

MANAGING ART EDITOR PHILIP GILDERDALE
SENIOR EDITOR MARTYN PAGE
MANAGING EDITOR RUTH MIDGLEY

PHOTOGRAPHY ANNA HODGSON, ANDY CRAWFORD
ILLUSTRATIONS COLIN ROSE, JOHN TEMPERTON
PRODUCTION JAYNE SIMPSON

This edition published in 1999 by Covent Garden Books

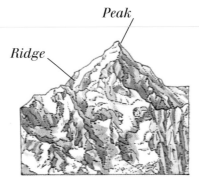

Peak

Ridge

MOUNTAIN

Rossby wave

Rossby wave becomes more developed

Fully developed Rossby wave

FORMATION OF ROSSBY WAVE IN THE JET STREAM

Water vapour forms clouds

Water evaporates from sea

River flows into sea

FIRST PUBLISHED IN GREAT BRITAIN IN 1993
BY DORLING KINDERSLEY LIMITED,
9 HENRIETTA STREET, LONDON WC2E 8PS
WWW.DK.COM

COPYRIGHT © 1993 DORLING KINDERSLEY LIMITED, LONDON

REPRINTED 1994

A CIP CATALOGUE RECORD FOR THIS BOOK IS AVAILABLE FROM THE BRITISH LIBRARY

ISBN 1-871-854-555

REPRODUCED BY COLOURSCAN, SINGAPORE
PRINTED AND BOUND BY ARTES GRÁFICAS TOLEDO, S.A.
D.L. TO: 608 - 1999

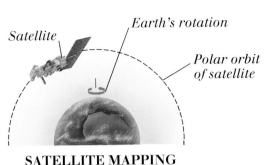

SATELLITE MAPPING OF THE EARTH

Satellite

Earth's rotation

Polar orbit of satellite

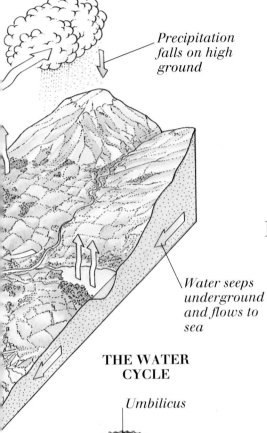

THE WATER CYCLE

Precipitation falls on high ground

Water seeps underground and flows to sea

Contents

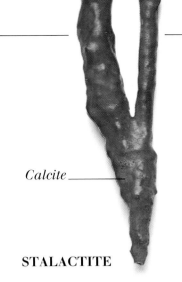

Calcite

STALACTITE

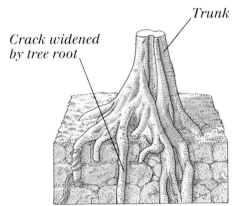

Trunk

Crack widened by tree root

TREE ROOT ACTION

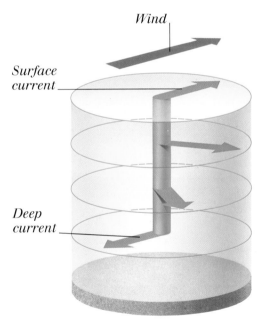

Wind

Surface current

Deep current

EKMAN SPIRAL (NORTHERN HEMISPHERE)

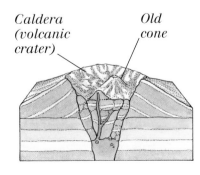

Caldera (volcanic crater)

Old cone

CALDERA VOLCANO

Umbilicus

Branching ribs

PAVLOVIA (AMMONITE MOLLUSC)

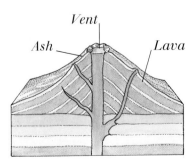

Vent

Ash

Lava

COMPOSITE VOLCANO

Planet Earth

THE EARTH

THE EARTH IS ONE OF THE NINE planets that orbit the Sun, which itself is just one of the approximately 100 billion stars in our galaxy – the Milky Way. Earth is the only planet that is known to support life. It is able to do so because it is the right distance from the Sun. If it were any nearer, conditions would be too hot for life; any farther away and it would be too cold. In addition, the Earth is the only planet known to have liquid water in large quantities. Its atmosphere helps to screen out some of the harmful radiation from the Sun, and also shields the planet from impacts by meteorites. The Earth consists of four main layers: an inner core, outer core, mantle, and crust. At the heart of the planet is the solid inner core, with a temperature of about 4,000°C. The heat from the inner core causes material in the molten outer core and mantle to circulate in convection currents. It is thought that these convection currents generate the Earth's magnetic field, which extends into space as the magnetosphere.

EARTH'S COORDINATE SYSTEM

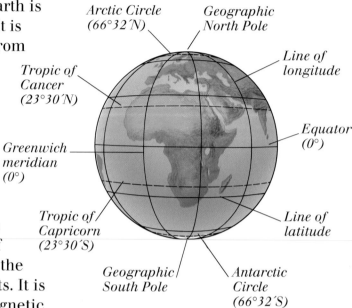

Arctic Circle (66°32´N)

Geographic North Pole

Line of longitude

Tropic of Cancer (23°30´N)

Equator (0°)

Greenwich meridian (0°)

Tropic of Capricorn (23°30´S)

Line of latitude

Geographic South Pole

Antarctic Circle (66°32´S)

EARTH'S PLACE IN THE SOLAR SYSTEM

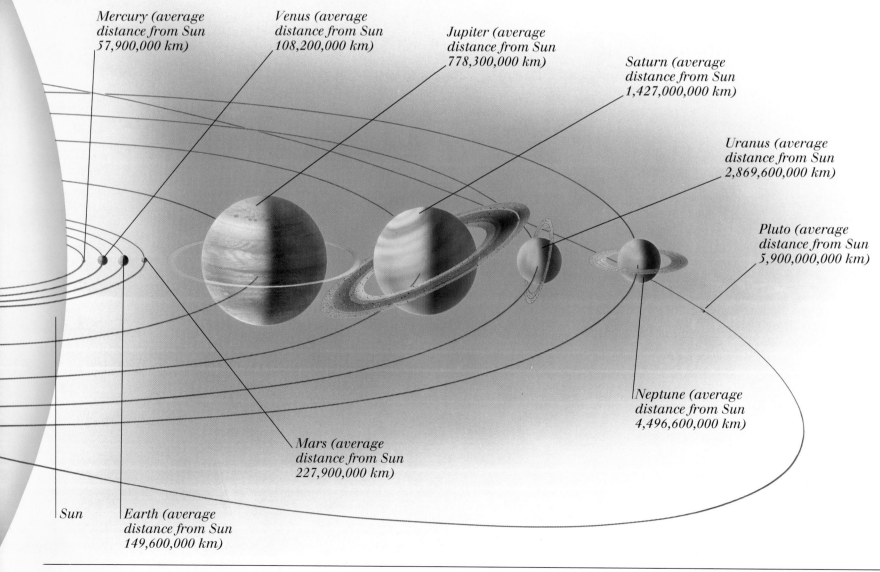

Mercury (average distance from Sun 57,900,000 km)

Venus (average distance from Sun 108,200,000 km)

Jupiter (average distance from Sun 778,300,000 km)

Saturn (average distance from Sun 1,427,000,000 km)

Uranus (average distance from Sun 2,869,600,000 km)

Pluto (average distance from Sun 5,900,000,000 km)

Neptune (average distance from Sun 4,496,600,000 km)

Mars (average distance from Sun 227,900,000 km)

Sun

Earth (average distance from Sun 149,600,000 km)

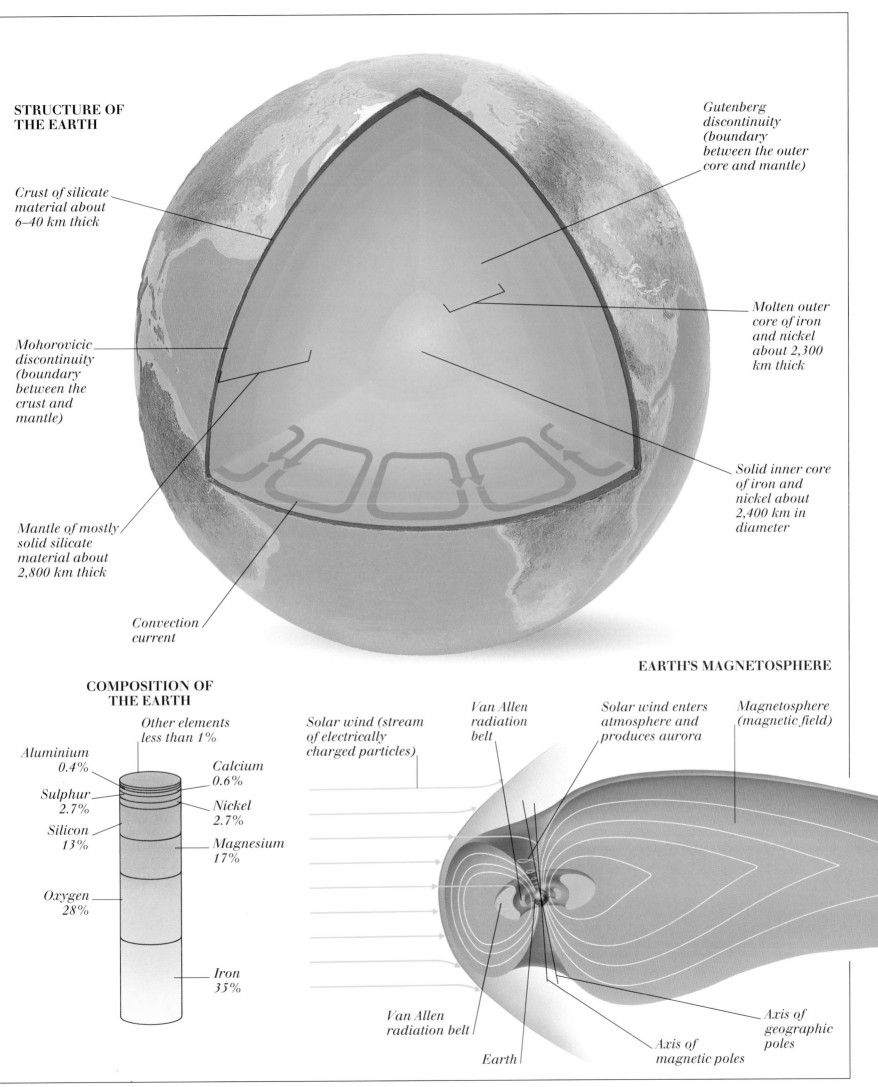

STRUCTURE OF THE EARTH

Crust of silicate material about 6–40 km thick

Mohorovicic discontinuity (boundary between the crust and mantle)

Mantle of mostly solid silicate material about 2,800 km thick

Convection current

Gutenberg discontinuity (boundary between the outer core and mantle)

Molten outer core of iron and nickel about 2,300 km thick

Solid inner core of iron and nickel about 2,400 km in diameter

COMPOSITION OF THE EARTH

Other elements less than 1%

Aluminium 0.4%

Calcium 0.6%

Sulphur 2.7%

Nickel 2.7%

Silicon 13%

Magnesium 17%

Oxygen 28%

Iron 35%

EARTH'S MAGNETOSPHERE

Solar wind (stream of electrically charged particles)

Van Allen radiation belt

Solar wind enters atmosphere and produces aurora

Magnetosphere (magnetic field)

Van Allen radiation belt

Earth

Axis of magnetic poles

Axis of geographic poles

Earth's physical features

MOST OF THE EARTH'S SURFACE (about 70 per cent) is covered with water. The largest single body of water, the Pacific Ocean, alone covers about 30 per cent of the surface. Most of the land is distributed as seven continents; these are (from largest to smallest) Asia, Africa, North America, South America, Antarctica, Europe, and Australasia. The physical features of the land are remarkably varied. Among the most notable are mountain ranges, rivers, and deserts. The largest mountain ranges – the Himalayas in Asia and the Andes in South America – extend for thousands of kilometres. The Himalayas include the world's highest mountain, Mount Everest (8,848 metres). The longest rivers are the River Nile in Africa (6,695 kilometres) and the Amazon River in South America (6,437 kilometres). Deserts cover about 20 per cent of the total land area. The largest is the Sahara, which covers nearly a third of Africa. The Earth's surface features can be represented in various ways. Only a globe can correctly represent areas, shapes, sizes, and directions, because there is always distortion when a spherical surface – the Earth's, for example – is projected on to the flat surface of a map. Each map projection is therefore a compromise: it shows some features accurately but distorts others. Even satellite mapping does not produce completely accurate maps, although they can show physical features with great clarity.

SATELLITE MAPPING OF THE EARTH

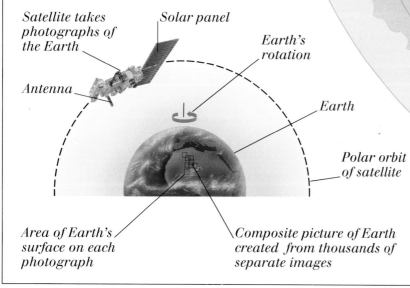

Satellite takes photographs of the Earth

Solar panel

Earth's rotation

Antenna

Earth

Polar orbit of satellite

Area of Earth's surface on each photograph

Composite picture of Earth created from thousands of separate images

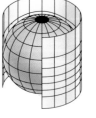

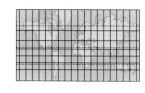

CYLINDRICAL PROJECTION

CYLINDRICAL-PROJECTION MAP

180°   160°   120°   80°

Great Slave Lake

Great Bear Lake

Lake Superior

Mackenzie-Peace River

Greenland

Bering Sea

Hudson Bay

Baffin Island

NORTH AMERICA

Rocky Mountains

Sonoran Desert

Lake Huron

Lake Ontario

Lake Erie

Lake Michigan

Sierra Madre

Chihuahuan Desert

Appalachian Mountains

ATLANTIC OCEAN

Gulf of Mexico

Mississippi-Missouri River

Caribbean Sea

Guiana Highlands

Amazon River

Brazilian Highlands

PACIFIC OCEAN

Andes

Atacama Desert

Gran Chaco

Mato Grosso

Parana River

Pampas

Patagonia

120°   80°

180°   160°

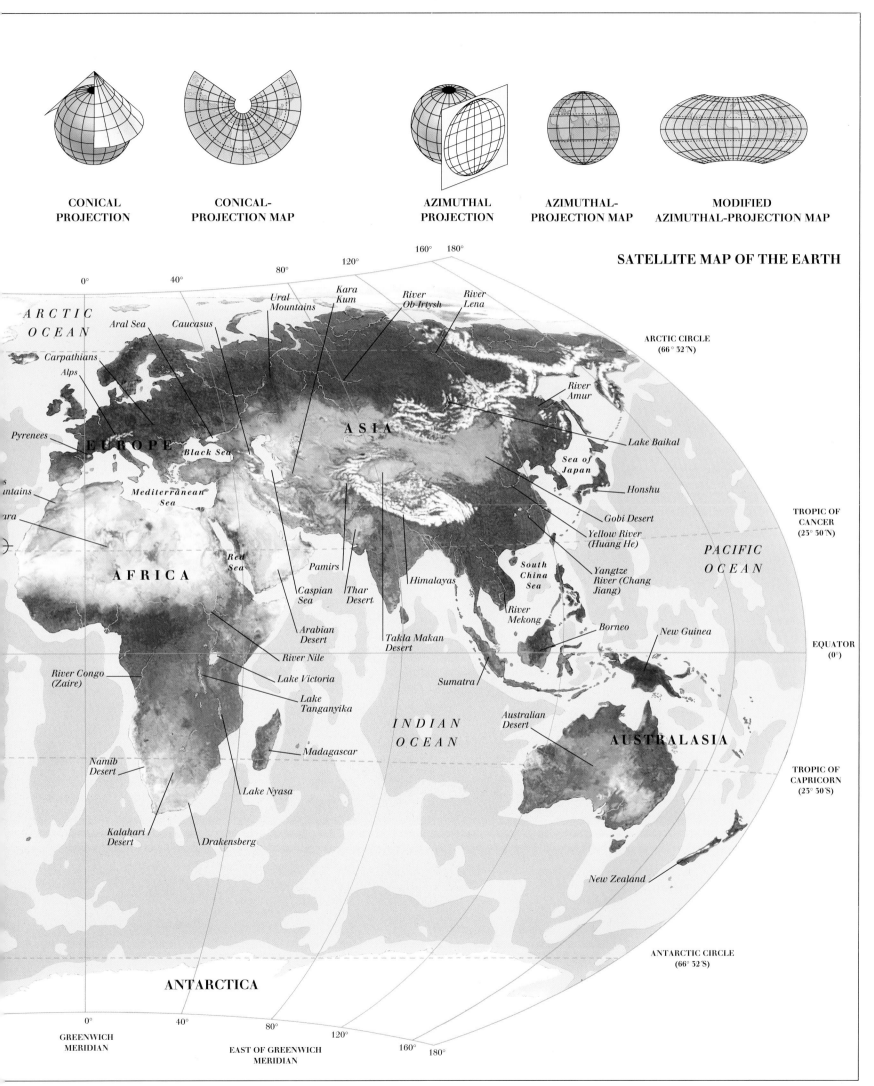

CONICAL
PROJECTION

CONICAL-
PROJECTION MAP

AZIMUTHAL
PROJECTION

AZIMUTHAL-
PROJECTION MAP

MODIFIED
AZIMUTHAL-PROJECTION MAP

SATELLITE MAP OF THE EARTH

160° 180°

120°

80°

40°

0°

*ARCTIC
OCEAN*

Ural
Mountains

Kara
Kum

River
Ob-Irtysh

River
Lena

ARCTIC CIRCLE
(66° 32´N)

Aral Sea

Caucasus

Carpathians

Alps

River
Amur

Pyrenees

E U R O P E

Black Sea

A S I A

Lake Baikal

Sea of
Japan

untains

*Mediterranean
Sea*

Gobi Desert

Honshu

TROPIC OF
CANCER
(25° 30´N)

ara

A F R I C A

*Red
Sea*

Pamirs

Thar
Desert

Himalayas

South
China
Sea

Yellow River
(Huang He)

Yangtze
River (Chang
Jiang)

*PACIFIC
OCEAN*

Caspian
Sea

River
Mekong

Borneo

New Guinea

Arabian
Desert

Takla Makan
Desert

EQUATOR
(0°)

River Nile

River Congo
(Zaire)

Lake Victoria

Sumatra

Lake
Tanganyika

*INDIAN
OCEAN*

Australian
Desert

AUSTRALASIA

Madagascar

Namib
Desert

Lake Nyasa

TROPIC OF
CAPRICORN
(25° 30´S)

Kalahari
Desert

Drakensberg

New Zealand

ANTARCTIC CIRCLE
(66° 32´S)

ANTARCTICA

0°

40°

80°

120°

160° 180°

GREENWICH
MERIDIAN

EAST OF GREENWICH
MERIDIAN

9

Geological time

THE EARTH FORMED FROM A CLOUD OF DUST and gas drifting through space about 4,600 million years ago. Dense minerals sank to the centre while lighter ones formed a thin rocky crust. However, the first known life-forms – bacteria and blue-green algae – did not appear until about 3,500 million years ago, and it was only about 570 million years ago that more complex plants and animals began to develop. Since then, thousands of animal and plant species have evolved; some have thrived and others, such as the dinosaurs, have died out. Like the species that inhabit it, the Earth itself is continually changing. The continents neared their present locations about 50 million years ago, but are still drifting slowly over the planet's surface, and mountain ranges such as the Himalayas – which began to form 40 million years ago – are continually being built up and worn away. Climate is also subject to change: the Earth has undergone a series of ice ages and glacial periods (the most recent glacial period occurred about 20,000 years ago) interspersed with warmer periods.

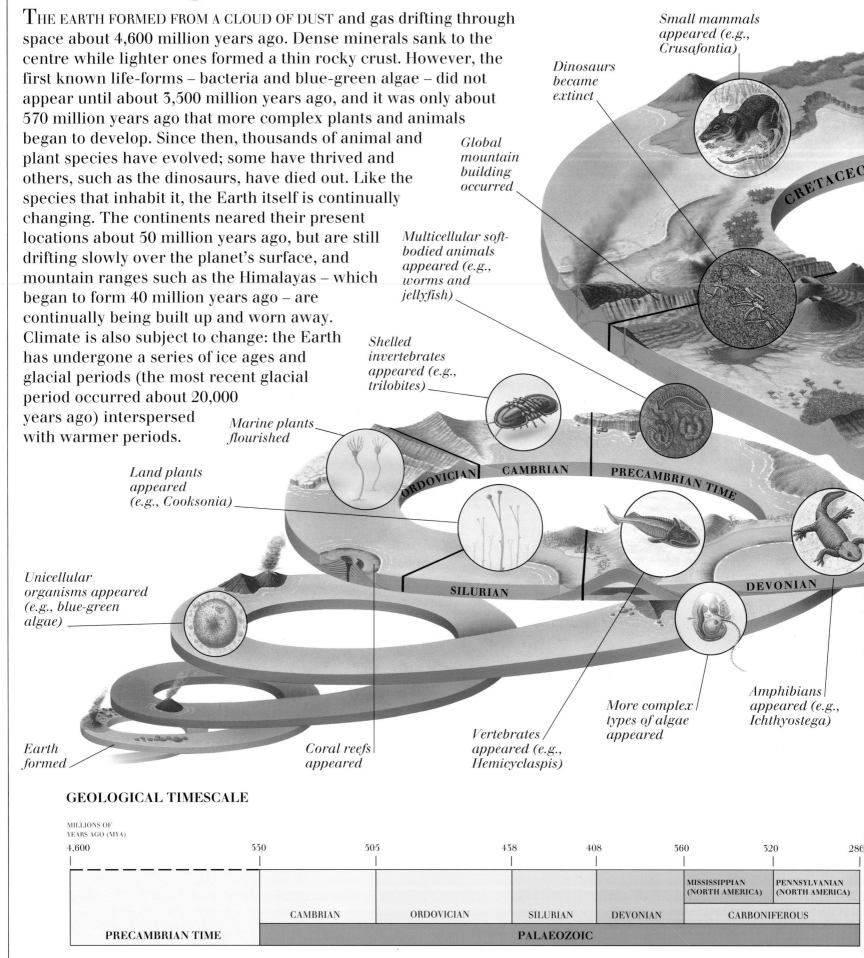

Small mammals appeared (e.g., Crusafontia)

Dinosaurs became extinct

Global mountain building occurred

Multicellular soft-bodied animals appeared (e.g., worms and jellyfish)

Shelled invertebrates appeared (e.g., trilobites)

Marine plants flourished

Land plants appeared (e.g., Cooksonia)

Unicellular organisms appeared (e.g., blue-green algae)

Earth formed

Coral reefs appeared

Vertebrates appeared (e.g., Hemicyclaspis)

More complex types of algae appeared

Amphibians appeared (e.g., Ichthyostega)

ORDOVICIAN · CAMBRIAN · PRECAMBRIAN TIME · SILURIAN · DEVONIAN · CRETACEO

GEOLOGICAL TIMESCALE

MILLIONS OF
YEARS AGO (MYA)

4,600	550	505	438	408	360	320	286

					MISSISSIPPIAN (NORTH AMERICA)	PENNSYLVANIAN (NORTH AMERICA)
	CAMBRIAN	ORDOVICIAN	SILURIAN	DEVONIAN	CARBONIFEROUS	
PRECAMBRIAN TIME	PALAEOZOIC					

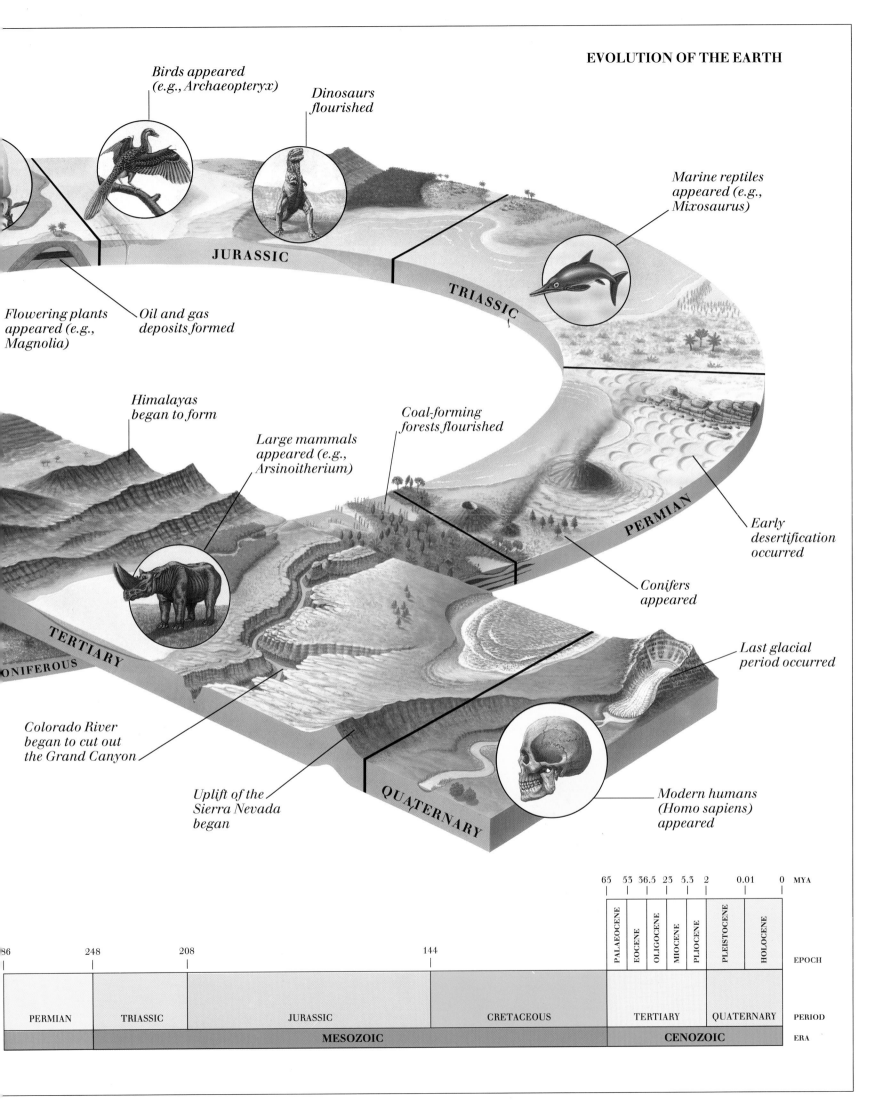

EVOLUTION OF THE EARTH

Birds appeared
(e.g., Archaeopteryx)

Dinosaurs
flourished

Marine reptiles
appeared (e.g.,
Mixosaurus)

JURASSIC

TRIASSIC

Flowering plants
appeared (e.g.,
Magnolia)

Oil and gas
deposits formed

Himalayas
began to form

Large mammals
appeared (e.g.,
Arsinoitherium)

Coal-forming
forests flourished

PERMIAN

Early
desertification
occurred

Conifers
appeared

Last glacial
period occurred

TERTIARY

ONIFEROUS

Colorado River
began to cut out
the Grand Canyon

Uplift of the
Sierra Nevada
began

QUATERNARY

Modern humans
(Homo sapiens)
appeared

					65	53	36.5	23	5.3	2		0.01		0	MYA
					PALAEOCENE	EOCENE	OLIGOCENE	MIOCENE	PLIOCENE		PLEISTOCENE		HOLOCENE		EPOCH
86	248	208		144											
PERMIAN	TRIASSIC	JURASSIC		CRETACEOUS				TERTIARY				QUATERNARY			PERIOD
			MESOZOIC							CENOZOIC					ERA

Earth's crust

THE EARTH'S CRUST IS THE SOLID OUTER shell of the Earth. It includes continental crust (about 40 kilometres thick) and oceanic crust (about six kilometres thick). The crust and the topmost layer of the mantle form the lithosphere. The lithosphere consists of semi-rigid plates that move relative to each other on the underlying asthenosphere (a partly molten layer of the mantle). This process is known as plate tectonics. Where two plates move apart, there are rifts in the crust. In mid-ocean, this movement results in sea-floor spreading and the formation of ocean ridges; on continents, crustal spreading can form rift valleys. When plates move towards each other, one may be subducted beneath (forced under) the other. In mid-ocean, this process results in ocean trenches, seismic activity, and arcs of volcanic islands. Mountains may be uplifted where oceanic crust is subducted beneath continental crust, or where continents collide (see pp. 16-17). Plates may also slide past each other – along the San Andreas fault, for example. Plate tectonics helps explain continental drift, the theory that the world's continents moved together about 175 million years ago to form a single landmass called Pangaea, which has subsequently split up.

Other elements 2%
Potassium 2.6%
Sodium 2.8%
Iron 5%
Magnesium 2%
Calcium 3.6%
Aluminium 8%
Silicon 28%
Oxygen 46%

FEATURES OF PLATE MOVEMENTS

Ridge where magma is rising
to form new oceanic crust

Ocean trench formed where
oceanic crust is forced
under continental crust

Subduction
zone

Region of
sea-floor
spreading

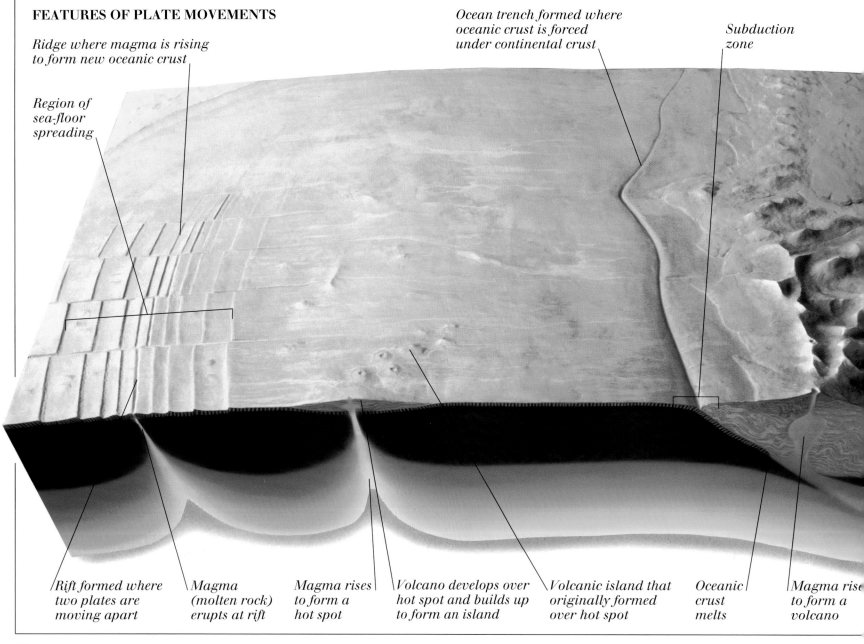

Rift formed where
two plates are
moving apart

Magma
(molten rock)
erupts at rift

Magma rises
to form a
hot spot

Volcano develops over
hot spot and builds up
to form an island

Volcanic island that
originally formed
over hot spot

Oceanic
crust
melts

Magma rise
to form a
volcano

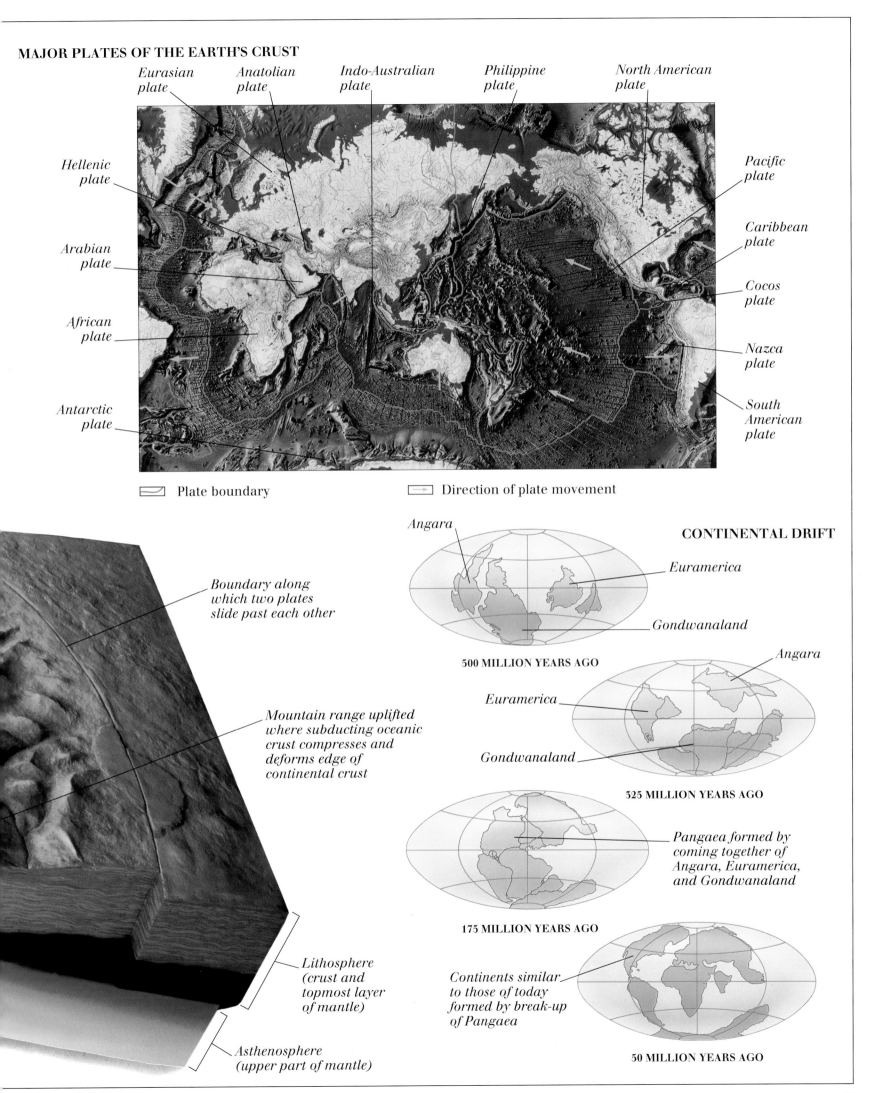

MAJOR PLATES OF THE EARTH'S CRUST

Eurasian plate

Anatolian plate

Indo-Australian plate

Philippine plate

North American plate

Hellenic plate

Arabian plate

African plate

Antarctic plate

Pacific plate

Caribbean plate

Cocos plate

Nazca plate

South American plate

⬜ Plate boundary

▭▶ Direction of plate movement

Boundary along which two plates slide past each other

Mountain range uplifted where subducting oceanic crust compresses and deforms edge of continental crust

Lithosphere (crust and topmost layer of mantle)

Asthenosphere (upper part of mantle)

CONTINENTAL DRIFT

Angara

Euramerica

Gondwanaland

500 MILLION YEARS AGO

Euramerica

Angara

Gondwanaland

525 MILLION YEARS AGO

Pangaea formed by coming together of Angara, Euramerica, and Gondwanaland

175 MILLION YEARS AGO

Continents similar to those of today formed by break-up of Pangaea

50 MILLION YEARS AGO

Faults and folds

THE CONTINUOUS MOVEMENT of the Earth's crustal plates (see pp. 12-13) can squeeze, stretch, or break rock strata, deforming them and producing faults and folds. A fault is a fracture in a rock along which there is movement of one side relative to the other. The movement can be vertical, horizontal, or oblique (vertical and horizontal). Faults develop when rocks are subjected to compression or tension. Faults tend to occur in hard, rigid rocks, which are more likely to break rather than bend. The smallest faults occur in single mineral crystals and are microscopically small, whereas the largest – the Great Rift Valley in Africa – is more than 9,000 kilometres long. Movement along faults is a common cause of earthquakes. A fold is a bend in a rock layer caused by compression. Folds occur in elastic rocks, which tend to bend rather than break. The two main types of folds are anticlines (upfolds) and synclines (downfolds). Folds vary in size from a few millimetres long to folded mountain ranges hundreds of kilometres long. In addition to faults and folds, other features associated with rock deformations include boudins, mullions, and *en échelon* fractures.

STRUCTURE OF A FOLD

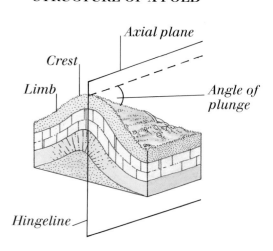

Axial plane

Crest

Limb

Angle of plunge

Hingeline

STRUCTURE OF A FAULT

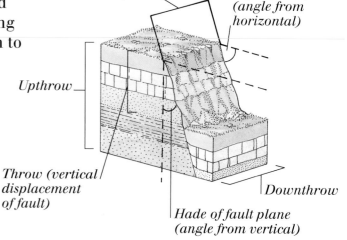

Fault plane

Dip of fault plane (angle from horizontal)

Upthrow

Throw (vertical displacement of fault)

Hade of fault plane (angle from vertical)

Downthrow

STRUCTURE OF A SLOPE

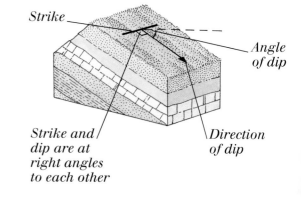

Strike

Angle of dip

Strike and dip are at right angles to each other

Direction of dip

FOLDED ROCK

Steeply dipping limbs

Crest of anticline

Plunge

SECTION THROUGH FOLDED ROCK STRATA THAT HAVE BEEN ERODED

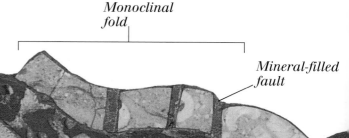

Dipping bed

Anticlinal fold

Monoclinal fold

Mineral-filled fault

Upper Carboniferous Millstone Grit

Lower Carboniferous Limestone

EXAMPLES OF FOLDS

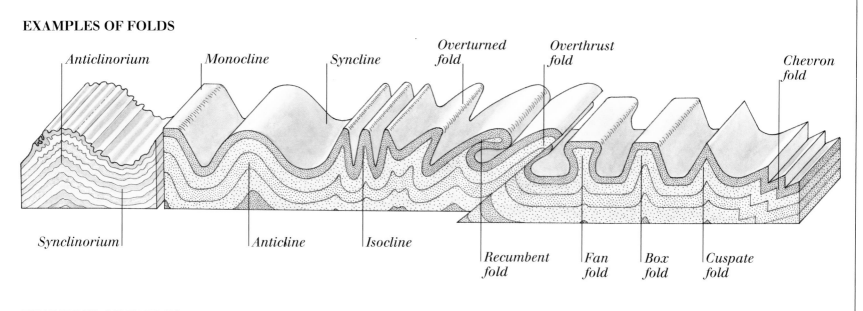

Anticlinorium
Monocline
Syncline
Overturned fold
Overthrust fold
Chevron fold
Synclinorium
Anticline
Isocline
Recumbent fold
Fan fold
Box fold
Cuspate fold

EXAMPLES OF FAULTS

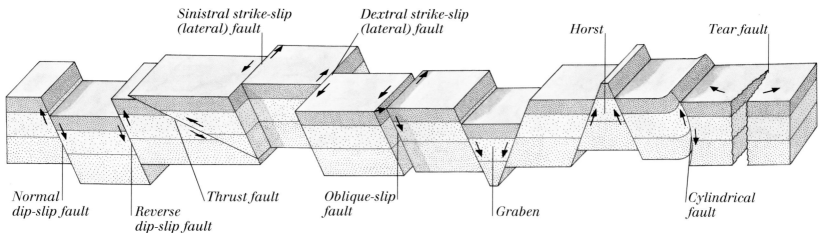

Sinistral strike-slip (lateral) fault
Dextral strike-slip (lateral) fault
Horst
Tear fault
Normal dip-slip fault
Reverse dip-slip fault
Thrust fault
Oblique-slip fault
Graben
Cylindrical fault

SMALL-SCALE ROCK DEFORMATIONS

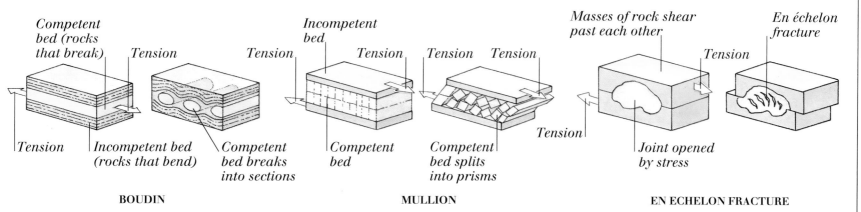

Competent bed (rocks that break)
Tension
Incompetent bed
Tension
Tension
Tension
Masses of rock shear past each other
Tension
En échelon fracture
Tension
Incompetent bed (rocks that bend)
Competent bed breaks into sections
Competent bed
Competent bed splits into prisms
Tension
Joint opened by stress

BOUDIN   **MULLION**   **EN ECHELON FRACTURE**

Mineral-filled fault
Dipping bed
Gently folded bed
Horizontal bed
Mineral-filled fault
Dipping bed

Upper Carboniferous Millstone Grit
Upper Carboniferous Coal Measures

Mountain building

THE PROCESSES INVOLVED in mountain building – termed orogenesis – occur as a result of the movement of the Earth's crustal plates (see pp. 12-13). There are three main types of mountains: volcanic mountains, fold mountains, and block mountains. Most volcanic mountains are formed along plate boundaries where plates come together or move apart (see pp. 18-19) and lava and other debris are ejected on to the Earth's surface. The lava and debris may build up to form a dome around the vent of a volcano. Fold mountains are formed where plates push together and cause the rock to buckle upwards. Where oceanic crust meets less dense continental crust, the oceanic crust is forced under the continental crust. The continental crust is buckled by the impact, and folded mountain ranges, such as the Appalachian Mountains in North America, are formed. Fold mountains are also formed where two areas of continental crust meet. The Himalayas, for example, began to form when India collided with Asia, buckling the sediments and parts of the oceanic crust between them. Block mountains are formed when a block of land is uplifted between two faults as a result of compression or tension in the Earth's crust (see pp. 14-15). Often, the movement along faults takes place gradually over millions of years. However, two plates may slide past each other suddenly along a faultline – the San Andreas fault, for example – causing earthquakes.

BHAGIRATHI PARBAT, HIMALAYAS

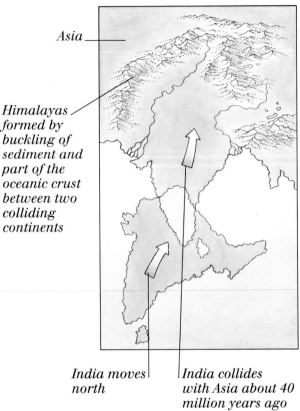

Asia

Himalayas formed by buckling of sediment and part of the oceanic crust between two colliding continents

India moves north

India collides with Asia about 40 million years ago

EXAMPLES OF MOUNTAINS

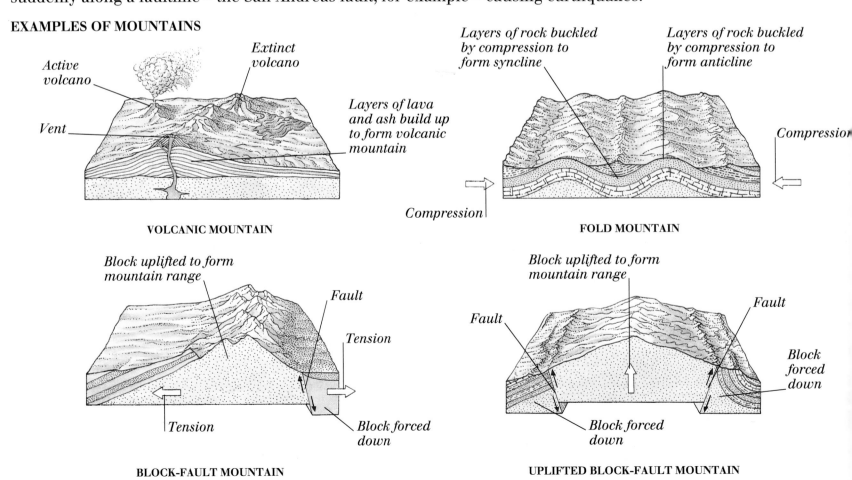

Active volcano

Extinct volcano

Vent

Layers of lava and ash build up to form volcanic mountain

VOLCANIC MOUNTAIN

Layers of rock buckled by compression to form syncline

Layers of rock buckled by compression to form anticline

Compression

Compression

FOLD MOUNTAIN

Block uplifted to form mountain range

Fault

Tension

Tension

Block forced down

BLOCK-FAULT MOUNTAIN

Block uplifted to form mountain range

Fault

Fault

Block forced down

Block forced down

UPLIFTED BLOCK-FAULT MOUNTAIN

STAGES IN THE FORMATION OF THE HIMALAYAS

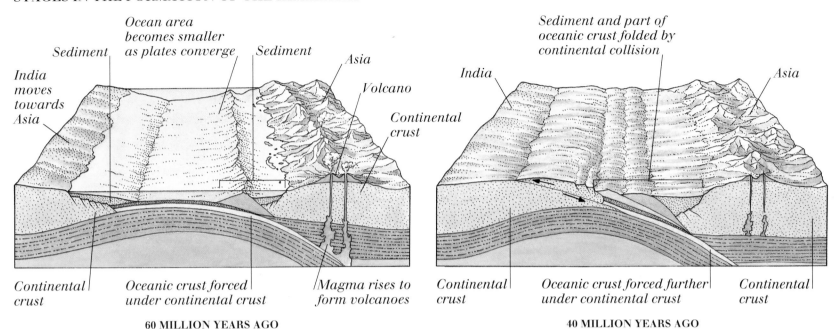

India moves towards Asia

Sediment

Ocean area becomes smaller as plates converge

Sediment

Asia

Volcano

Continental crust

Continental crust

Oceanic crust forced under continental crust

Magma rises to form volcanoes

60 MILLION YEARS AGO

Sediment and part of oceanic crust folded by continental collision

India

Asia

Continental crust

Oceanic crust forced further under continental crust

Continental crust

40 MILLION YEARS AGO

Ganges plain

Sediment and part of oceanic crust folded and uplifted

India

Asia

Continental crust

Continental crust

20 MILLION YEARS AGO

Sediment and part of oceanic crust further folded and uplifted to form Himalayas

Ripple effect of collision forms mountains and plateau of Tibet

Ganges plain

India

Asia

Continental crust

Continental crust

TODAY

SAN ANDREAS FAULT

Faultline along which two plates may slide past each other, causing an earthquake

EARTHQUAKES

Epicentre (point on Earth's surface directly above focus)

Shock waves radiate outwards from focus

Isoseismal lines join places with equal intensity of shock

Focus (point at which earthquake originates)

ANATOMY OF AN EARTHQUAKE

Core (blocks S waves and deflects P waves)

Focus

Crust

S and P shock waves

L wave

Mantle

P wave shadow zone

P wave shadow zone

P wave

PATH OF SHOCK WAVES THROUGH THE EARTH

17

Volcanoes

VOLCANOES ARE VENTS OR FISSURES in the Earth's crust through which magma (molten rock that originates from deep beneath the crust) is forced on to the surface as lava. They occur most commonly along the boundaries of crustal plates; most volcanoes lie in a belt called the "Ring of Fire", which runs along the edge of the Pacific Ocean. Volcanoes can be classified according to the violence and frequency of their eruptions. Non-explosive volcanic eruptions generally occur where crustal plates pull apart. These eruptions produce runny basaltic lava that spreads quickly over a wide area to form relatively flat cones. The most violent eruptions take place where plates collide. Such eruptions produce thick rhyolitic lava and may also blast out clouds of dust and pyroclasts (lava fragments). The lava does not flow far before cooling and therefore builds up steep-sided, conical volcanoes. Some volcanoes produce lava and ash eruptions, which build up composite volcanic cones. Volcanoes that erupt frequently are described as active; those that erupt rarely are termed dormant; and those that have stopped erupting altogether are termed extinct. As well as the volcanoes themselves, other features associated with volcanic regions include geysers, hot mineral springs, solfataras, fumaroles, and bubbling mud pools.

Folded, rope-like surface

PAHOEHOE
(ROPY LAVA)

HORU GEYSER,
NEW ZEALAND

VOLCANO TYPES

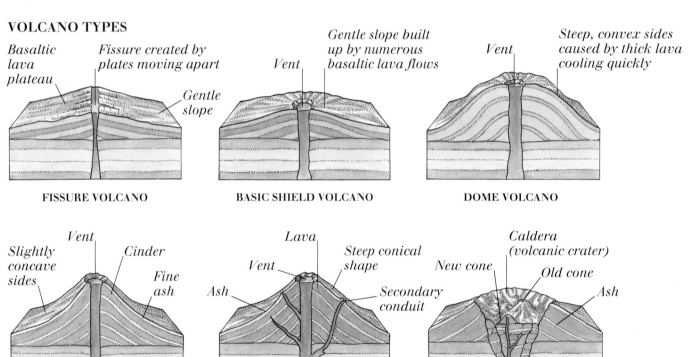

Basaltic lava plateau — *Fissure created by plates moving apart* — *Gentle slope*

FISSURE VOLCANO

Gentle slope built up by numerous basaltic lava flows — *Vent*

BASIC SHIELD VOLCANO

Vent — *Steep, convex sides caused by thick lava cooling quickly*

DOME VOLCANO

Slightly concave sides — *Vent* — *Cinder* — *Fine ash*

ASH-CINDER VOLCANO

Lava — *Vent* — *Steep conical shape* — *Ash* — *Secondary conduit*

COMPOSITE VOLCANO

Caldera (volcanic crater) — *New cone* — *Old cone* — *Ash*

CALDERA VOLCANO

HOW VOLCANIC PLUGS BECOME EXPOSED

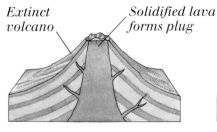

Extinct volcano — *Solidified lava forms plug*

PLUG FORMATION

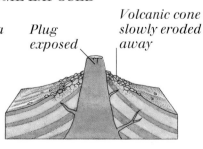

Plug exposed — *Volcanic cone slowly eroded away*

INITIAL EROSION AROUND PLUG

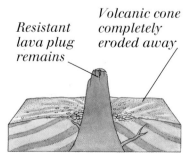

Resistant lava plug remains — *Volcanic cone completely eroded away*

COMPLETE DENUDATION OF PLUG

**LAPILLI
(LAVA FRAGMENTS)**

Small piece of solidified lava

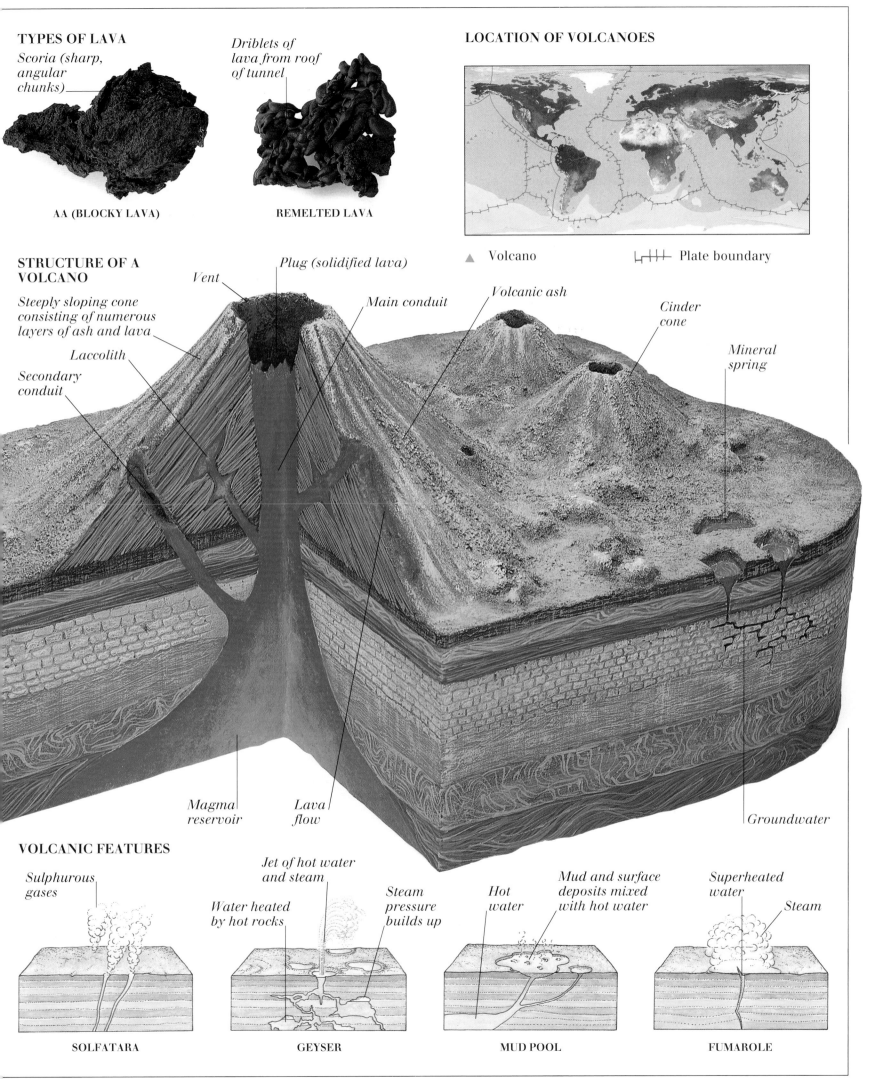

TYPES OF LAVA

Scoria (sharp, angular chunks)

Driblets of lava from roof of tunnel

AA (BLOCKY LAVA)

REMELTED LAVA

LOCATION OF VOLCANOES

▲ Volcano

⊢┼┼┼ Plate boundary

STRUCTURE OF A VOLCANO

Steeply sloping cone consisting of numerous layers of ash and lava

Laccolith

Secondary conduit

Vent

Plug (solidified lava)

Main conduit

Volcanic ash

Cinder cone

Mineral spring

Magma reservoir

Lava flow

Groundwater

VOLCANIC FEATURES

Sulphurous gases

Jet of hot water and steam

Water heated by hot rocks

Steam pressure builds up

Hot water

Mud and surface deposits mixed with hot water

Superheated water

Steam

SOLFATARA

GEYSER

MUD POOL

FUMAROLE

19

The rock cycle

THE ROCK CYCLE IS A CONTINUOUS PROCESS through which old rocks are transformed into new ones. Rocks can be divided into three main groups: igneous, sedimentary, and metamorphic. Igneous rocks are formed when magma (molten rock) from the Earth's interior cools and solidifies (see pp. 26-27). Sedimentary rocks are formed when sediment (rock particles, for example) becomes compressed and cemented together in a process known as lithification (see pp. 28-29). Metamorphic rocks are formed when igneous, sedimentary, or other metamorphic rocks are changed by heat or pressure (see pp. 26-27). Rocks are added to the Earth's surface by crustal movements and volcanic activity. Once exposed on the surface, the rocks are broken down into rock particles by weathering (see pp. 34-35). The particles are then transported by glaciers, rivers, and wind, and deposited as sediment in lakes, deltas, deserts, and on the ocean floor. Some of this sediment undergoes lithification and forms sedimentary rock. This rock may be thrust back to the surface by crustal movements or forced deeper into the Earth's interior, where heat and pressure transform it into metamorphic rock. The metamorphic rock in turn may be pushed up to the surface or may be melted to form magma. Eventually, the magma cools and solidifies – below or on the surface – forming igneous rock. When the sedimentary, igneous, and metamorphic rocks are exposed once more on the Earth's surface, the cycle begins again.

HEXAGONAL BASALT
COLUMNS, ICELAND

THE ROCK CYCLE

Igneous rock

Cooling and solidification (crystallization)

Weathering, transport, and deposition

Sediment

Heat and pressure (metamorphism)

Weathering, transport, and deposition

Weathering, transport, and deposition

Compression and cementation (lithification)

Magma

Melting

Heat and pressure (metamorphism)

Metamorphic rock

Sedimentary rock

STAGES IN THE ROCK CYCLE

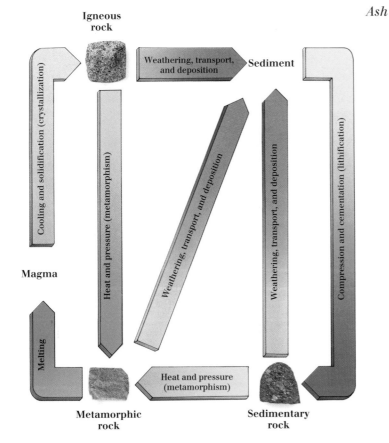

Magma extruded as lava, which solidifies to form igneous rock

Lava flow

Vent

Main conduit

Secondary conduit

Lava

Ash

Rock surrounding magma changed by heat to form metamorphic rock

Intense heat of rising magma melts some of the surrounding rock

Sedimentary rock crushed and folded to form metamorphic rock

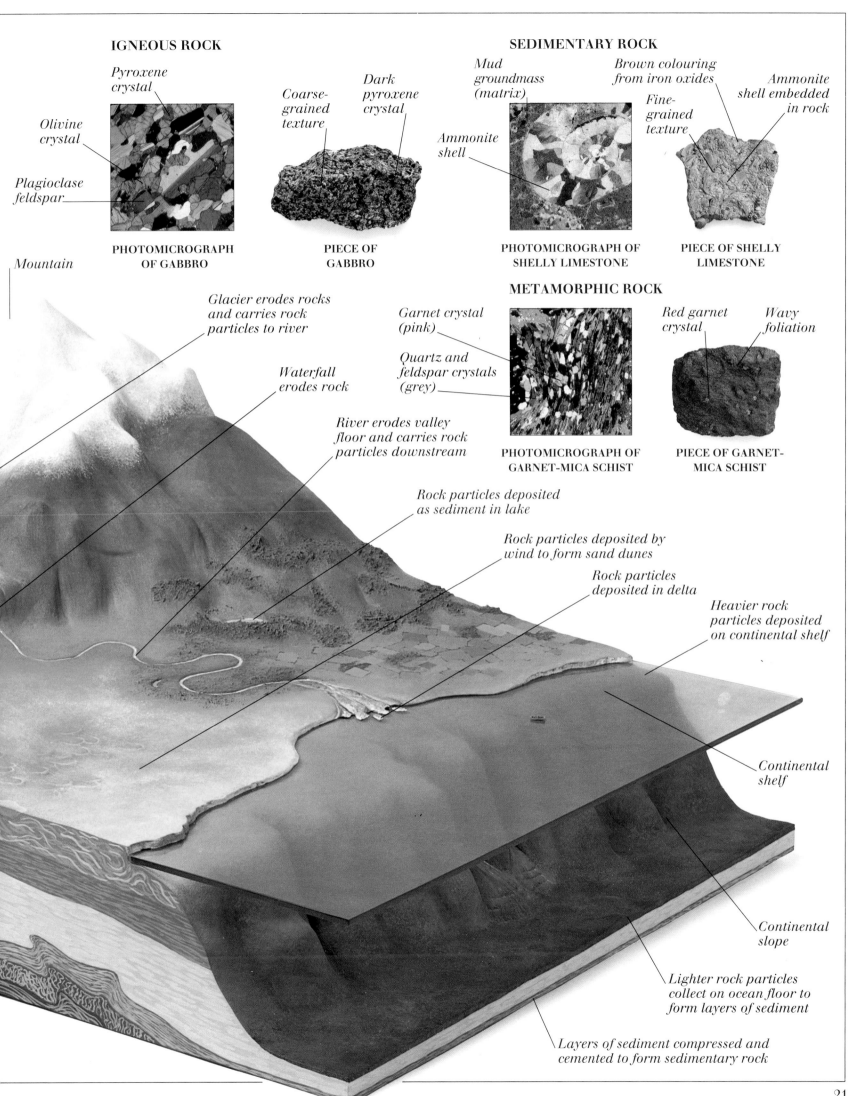

IGNEOUS ROCK

Pyroxene crystal

Olivine crystal

Plagioclase feldspar

PHOTOMICROGRAPH OF GABBRO

Coarse-grained texture

Dark pyroxene crystal

PIECE OF GABBRO

SEDIMENTARY ROCK

Mud groundmass (matrix)

Ammonite shell

Brown colouring from iron oxides

Fine-grained texture

Ammonite shell embedded in rock

PHOTOMICROGRAPH OF SHELLY LIMESTONE

PIECE OF SHELLY LIMESTONE

METAMORPHIC ROCK

Garnet crystal (pink)

Quartz and feldspar crystals (grey)

Red garnet crystal

Wavy foliation

PHOTOMICROGRAPH OF GARNET-MICA SCHIST

PIECE OF GARNET-MICA SCHIST

Mountain

Glacier erodes rocks and carries rock particles to river

Waterfall erodes rock

River erodes valley floor and carries rock particles downstream

Rock particles deposited as sediment in lake

Rock particles deposited by wind to form sand dunes

Rock particles deposited in delta

Heavier rock particles deposited on continental shelf

Continental shelf

Continental slope

Lighter rock particles collect on ocean floor to form layers of sediment

Layers of sediment compressed and cemented to form sedimentary rock

Minerals

A MINERAL IS A NATURALLY OCCURRING SUBSTANCE that has a characteristic chemical composition and specific physical properties, such as habit and streak (see pp. 24-25). A rock, by comparison, is an aggregate of minerals and need not have a specific chemical composition. Minerals are made up of elements (substances that cannot be broken down chemically into simpler substances), each of which can be represented by a chemical symbol (see p. 58). Minerals can be divided into two main groups: native elements and compounds. Native elements are made up of a pure element. Examples include gold (chemical symbol Au), silver (Ag), copper (Cu), and carbon (C); carbon occurs as a native element in two forms, diamond and graphite. Compounds are combinations of two or more elements. For example, sulphides are compounds of sulphur (S) and one or more other elements, such as lead (Pb) in the mineral galena, or antimony (Sb) in the mineral stibnite.

NATIVE ELEMENTS

Dendritic (branching) copper

Limonite groundmass (matrix)

COPPER
(Cu)

SULPHIDES

Cubic galena crystal

GALENA
(PbS)

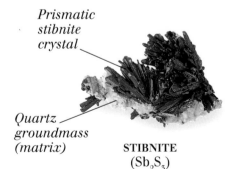

Prismatic stibnite crystal

Quartz groundmass (matrix)

STIBNITE
(Sb_2S_3)

Perfect octahedral pyrites crystal

Quartz crystal

PYRITES
(FeS_2)

Dendritic (branching) gold

Quartz vein

GOLD
(Au)

White diamond

Kimberlite groundmass (matrix)

DIAMOND
(C)

Hexagonal graphite crystal

GRAPHITE
(C)

OXIDES/HYDROXIDES

Milky quartz groundmass (matrix)

Smoky quartz crystal

SMOKY QUARTZ
(SiO_2)

Rounded bauxite grains in groundmass (matrix)

BAUXITE
(FeO(OH) and $Al_2O_3.2H_2O$)

Mass of specular haematite crystals

SPECULAR HAEMATITE
(Fe_2O_3)

Parallel bands of onyx

ONYX
(SiO_2)

Kidney ore haematite

Specular crystals of haematite

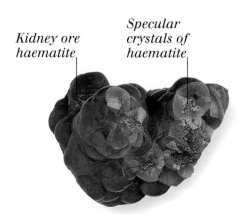

KIDNEY ORE HAEMATITE
(Fe_2O_3)

PHOSPHATES

Limonite groundmass (matrix)

Rock groundmass (matrix)

Radiating wavellite crystals

Prismatic pyromorphite crystals

WAVELLITE
$(Al_5(PO_4)_2(OH,F)_3.5H_2O)$

PYROMORPHITE
$(Pb_5(PO_4)_3Cl)$

CARBONATES

Striated cerussite crystal

Dog-tooth calcite crystal

CERUSSITE
$(PbCO_3)$

CALCITE
$(CaCO_3)$

SULPHATES

Rock groundmass (matrix)

Radiating crystal mass of daisy gypsum

Radiating cyanotrichite crystals

CYANOTRICHITE
$(Cu_4Al_2(SO_4)(OH)_{12}.2H_2O)$

DAISY GYPSUM
$(CaSO_4.2H_2O)$

MOLYBDATE

Tabular wulfenite crystal

Dark rock groundmass (matrix)

WULFENITE
$(PbMoO_4)$

SILICATES

Feldspar groundmass (matrix)

Transparent bicoloured tourmaline crystal

Dodecahedral sodalite crystal

SODALITE
$(Na_8Al_6Si_6O_{24}Cl_2)$

Striated surface of olivine crystal

TOURMALINE
$(Na(Mg,Fe,Li,Mn,Al)_3Al_6(BO_3)_3Si_6.O_{18}(OH,F)_4)$

OLIVINE
$(Fe_2SiO_4 - Mg_2SiO_4)$

Striated prismatic epidote crystal

Tabular muscovite crystal

EPIDOTE
$(Ca_2(Al,Fe)_3(SiO_4)_3(OH))$

Orthoclase crystal

MUSCOVITE
$(KAl_2(Si_3Al)O_{10}(OH,F)_2)$

ORTHOCLASE
$(KAlSi_3O_8)$

HALIDES

Cubic rock salt crystal

Cubic fluorite crystal

GREEN FLUORITE
(CaF_2)

ORANGE HALITE (ROCK SALT)
$(NaCl)$

Mineral features

MINERALS CAN BE IDENTIFIED BY STUDYING features such as fracture, cleavage, crystal system, habit, hardness, colour, and streak. Minerals can break in different ways. If a mineral breaks in an irregular way, leaving rough surfaces, it possesses fracture. If a mineral breaks along well-defined planes of weakness, it possesses cleavage. Specific minerals have distinctive patterns of cleavage; for example, mica cleaves along one plane. Most minerals form crystals, which can be categorized into crystal systems according to their symmetry and number of faces. Within each system, several different but related forms of crystal are possible; for example, a cubic crystal can have six, eight, or twelve sides. A mineral's habit is the typical form taken by an aggregate of its crystals. Examples of habit include botryoidal (like a bunch of grapes) and massive (no definite form). The relative hardness of a mineral may be assessed by testing its resistance to scratching. This property is usually measured using Mohs scale, which increases in hardness from 1 (talc) to 10 (diamond). The colour of a mineral is not a dependable guide to its identity as some minerals have a range of colours. Streak (the colour the powdered mineral makes when rubbed across an unglazed tile) is a more reliable indicator.

CLEAVAGE

Cleavage in one direction

CLEAVAGE ALONG ONE PLANE

Cleavage in three directions, forming a block cube

CLEAVAGE ALONG THREE PLANES
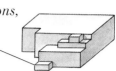

Horizontal cleavage

Vertical cleavage

CLEAVAGE ALONG TWO PLANES

Cleavage in four directions, forming a double-pyramid crystal

CLEAVAGE ALONG FOUR PLANES

CRYSTAL SYSTEMS

Cubic iron pyrites crystal

CUBIC SYSTEM

Representation of cubic system

Tetragonal idocrase crystal

Representation of tetragonal system

TETRAGONAL SYSTEM
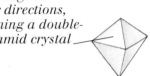

Hexagonal beryl crystal

Representation of hexagonal/ trigonal system

HEXAGONAL/TRIGONAL SYSTEM

Orthorhombic barytes crystal

Representation of orthorhombic system

ORTHORHOMBIC SYSTEM

FRACTURE

Fire opal with conchoidal (shell-like) fracture

CONCHOIDAL FRACTURE

Nickel-iron with hackly (jagged) fracture

HACKLY FRACTURE

Orpiment with uneven fracture

UNEVEN FRACTURE

Garnierite with splintery fracture

SPLINTERY FRACTURE

Monoclinic selenite crystal

Representation of monoclinic system

MONOCLINIC SYSTEM

Representation of triclinic system

Triclinic axinite crystal

TRICLINIC SYSTEM
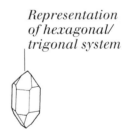

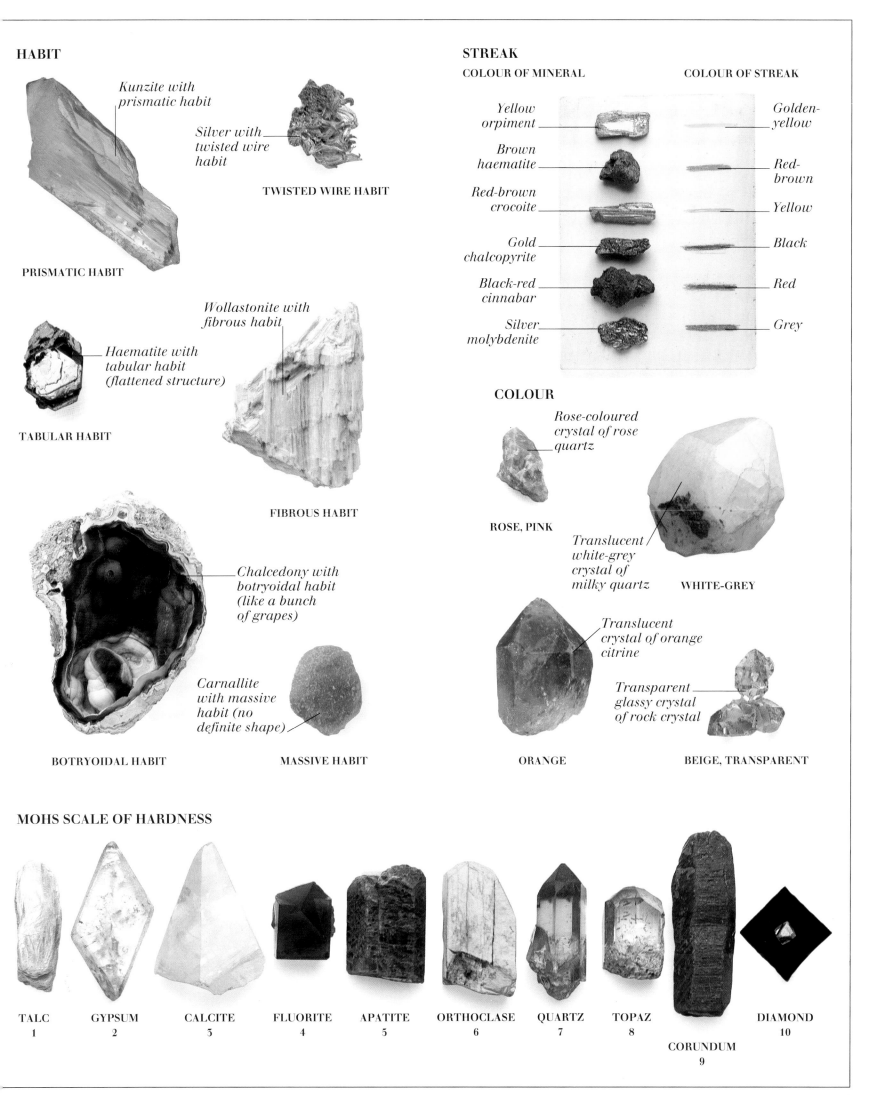

HABIT

Kunzite with prismatic habit

Silver with twisted wire habit

TWISTED WIRE HABIT

PRISMATIC HABIT

Wollastonite with fibrous habit

Haematite with tabular habit (flattened structure)

TABULAR HABIT

FIBROUS HABIT

Chalcedony with botryoidal habit (like a bunch of grapes)

Carnallite with massive habit (no definite shape)

BOTRYOIDAL HABIT

MASSIVE HABIT

STREAK

COLOUR OF MINERAL

COLOUR OF STREAK

Yellow orpiment

Golden-yellow

Brown haematite

Red-brown

Red-brown crocoite

Yellow

Gold chalcopyrite

Black

Black-red cinnabar

Red

Silver molybdenite

Grey

COLOUR

Rose-coloured crystal of rose quartz

ROSE, PINK

Translucent white-grey crystal of milky quartz

WHITE-GREY

Translucent crystal of orange citrine

Transparent glassy crystal of rock crystal

ORANGE

BEIGE, TRANSPARENT

MOHS SCALE OF HARDNESS

TALC	GYPSUM	CALCITE	FLUORITE	APATITE	ORTHOCLASE	QUARTZ	TOPAZ	CORUNDUM	DIAMOND
1	2	3	4	5	6	7	8	9	10

Igneous and metamorphic rocks

IGNEOUS ROCKS ARE FORMED WHEN MAGMA (molten rock that originates from deep beneath the Earth's crust) cools and solidifies. There are two main types of igneous rock: intrusive and extrusive. Intrusive rocks are formed deep underground where magma is forced into cracks or between rock layers to form structures such as sills, dykes, and batholiths. The magma cools slowly to form coarse-grained rocks such as gabbro and pegmatite. Extrusive rocks are formed above the Earth's surface from lava (magma that has been ejected in a volcanic eruption). The molten lava cools quickly, producing fine-grained rocks such as rhyolite and basalt. Metamorphic rocks are those that have been altered by intense heat (contact metamorphism) or extreme pressure (regional metamorphism). Contact metamorphism occurs when rocks are changed by heat from, for example, an igneous intrusion or lava flow. Regional metamorphism occurs when rock is crushed in the middle of a folding mountain range. Metamorphic rocks can be formed from igneous rocks, sedimentary rocks, or even from other metamorphic rocks.

Cinder cone

Large eroded lava flow

Cedar-tree laccolith

Butte

Plug

Cone sheet

Ring dyke

Batholith

Dyke

Sill

Dyke swarm

Lopolith

IGNEOUS ROCK STRUCTURES

CONTACT METAMORPHISM

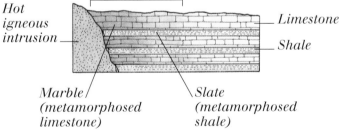

Metamorphic aureole (region where contact metamorphism occurs)

Hot igneous intrusion

Limestone

Shale

Marble (metamorphosed limestone)

Slate (metamorphosed shale)

REGIONAL METAMORPHISM

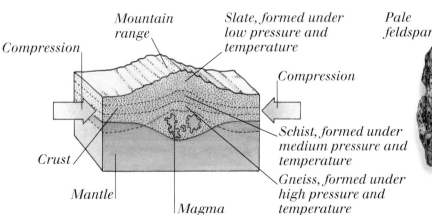

Mountain range

Slate, formed under low pressure and temperature

Compression

Compression

Schist, formed under medium pressure and temperature

Gneiss, formed under high pressure and temperature

Crust

Mantle

Magma

EXAMPLES OF METAMORPHIC ROCKS

Pale feldspar

Dark mica

Dark mineral band

Pale calcite

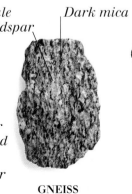

GNEISS

FOLDED SCHIST

SKARN

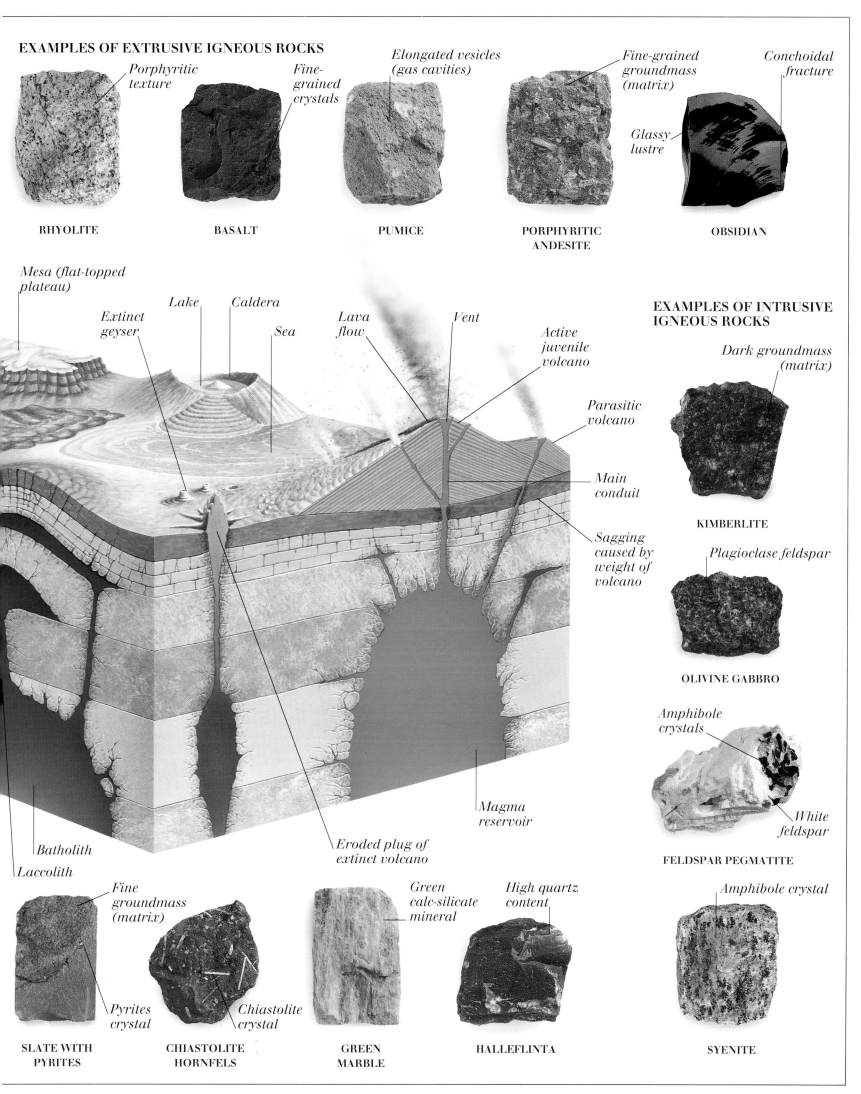

EXAMPLES OF EXTRUSIVE IGNEOUS ROCKS

Porphyritic texture

Fine-grained crystals

Elongated vesicles (gas cavities)

Fine-grained groundmass (matrix)

Conchoidal fracture

Glassy lustre

RHYOLITE

BASALT

PUMICE

PORPHYRITIC ANDESITE

OBSIDIAN

Mesa (flat-topped plateau)

Extinct geyser

Lake

Caldera

Sea

Lava flow

Vent

Active juvenile volcano

Parasitic volcano

Main conduit

Sagging caused by weight of volcano

Batholith

Laccolith

Eroded plug of extinct volcano

Magma reservoir

EXAMPLES OF INTRUSIVE IGNEOUS ROCKS

Dark groundmass (matrix)

KIMBERLITE

Plagioclase feldspar

OLIVINE GABBRO

Amphibole crystals

White feldspar

FELDSPAR PEGMATITE

Fine groundmass (matrix)

Pyrites crystal

Chiastolite crystal

SLATE WITH PYRITES

CHIASTOLITE HORNFELS

Green calc-silicate mineral

High quartz content

Amphibole crystal

GREEN MARBLE

HALLEFLINTA

SYENITE

Sedimentary rocks

SEDIMENTARY ROCKS ARE FORMED BY THE ACCUMULATION and consolidation of sediments (see pp. 20-21). There are three main types of sedimentary rock. Clastic sedimentary rocks, such as breccia or sandstone, are formed from other rocks that have been broken down into fragments by weathering (see pp. 34-35), which have then been transported and deposited elsewhere. Organic sedimentary rocks – for example, coal (see pp. 32-33) – are derived from plant and animal remains. Chemical sedimentary rocks are formed by chemical processes. For example, rock salt is formed when salt dissolved in water is deposited as the water evaporates. Sedimentary rocks are laid down in layers, called beds or strata. Each new layer is laid down horizontally over older ones. There are usually some gaps in the sequence, called unconformities. These represent periods in which no new sediments were being laid down, or when earlier sedimentary layers were raised above sea level and eroded away.

THE GRAND CANYON, USA

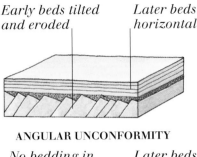

Early beds tilted and eroded   *Later beds horizontal*

ANGULAR UNCONFORMITY

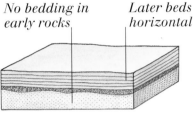

No bedding in early rocks   *Later beds horizontal*

NONCONFORMITY

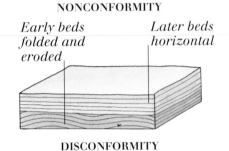

Early beds folded and eroded   *Later beds horizontal*

DISCONFORMITY

SEDIMENTARY LAYERS OF THE GRAND CANYON REGION

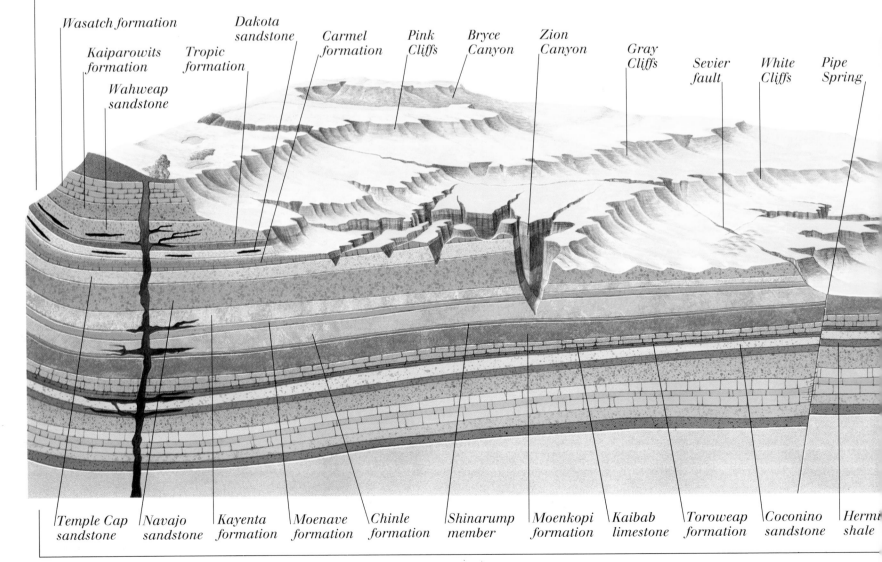

Wasatch formation

Kaiparowits formation

Tropic formation

Wahweap sandstone

Dakota sandstone

Carmel formation

Pink Cliffs

Bryce Canyon

Zion Canyon

Gray Cliffs

Sevier fault

White Cliffs

Pipe Spring

Temple Cap sandstone   *Navajo sandstone*   *Kayenta formation*   *Moenave formation*   *Chinle formation*   *Shinarump member*   *Moenkopi formation*   *Kaibab limestone*   *Toroweap formation*   *Coconino sandstone*   *Hermit shale*

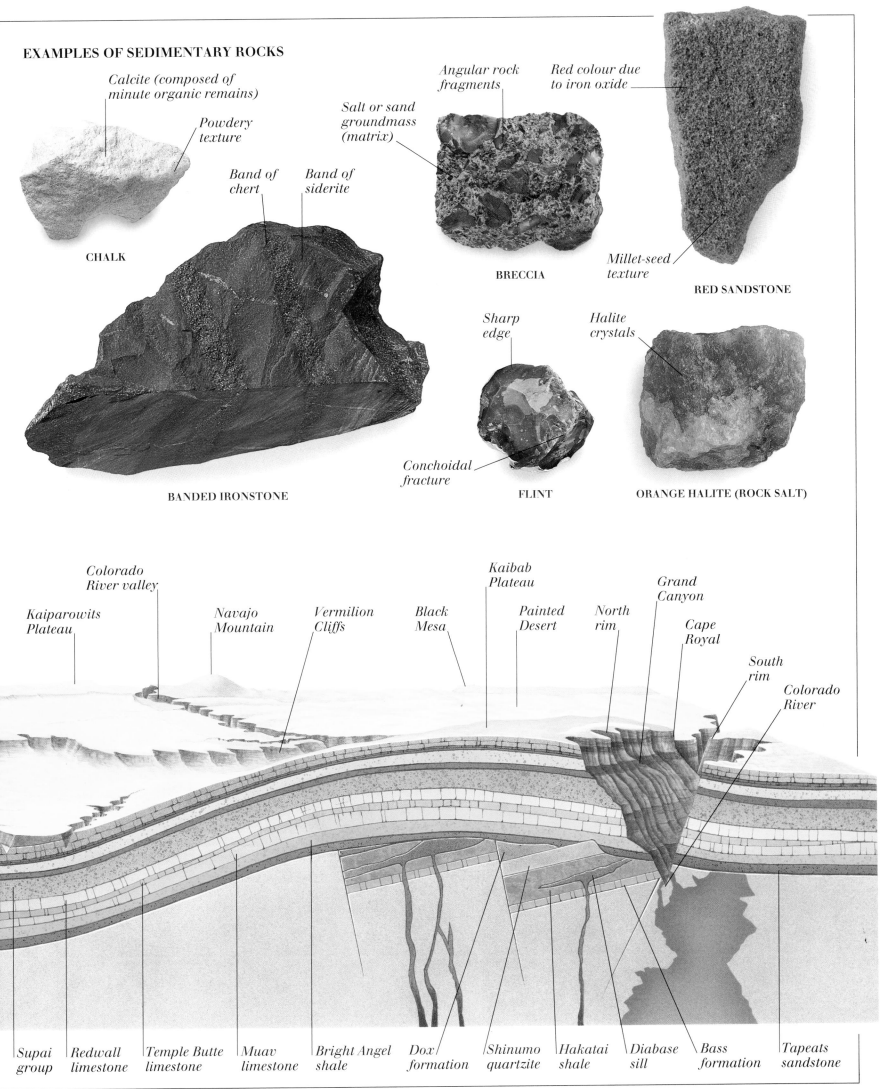

EXAMPLES OF SEDIMENTARY ROCKS

Calcite (composed of minute organic remains)

Powdery texture

CHALK

Band of chert

Band of siderite

BANDED IRONSTONE

Angular rock fragments

Salt or sand groundmass (matrix)

BRECCIA

Red colour due to iron oxide

Millet-seed texture

RED SANDSTONE

Sharp edge

Conchoidal fracture

FLINT

Halite crystals

ORANGE HALITE (ROCK SALT)

Kaiparowits Plateau

Colorado River valley

Navajo Mountain

Vermilion Cliffs

Black Mesa

Kaibab Plateau

Painted Desert

North rim

Grand Canyon

Cape Royal

South rim

Colorado River

Supai group

Redwall limestone

Temple Butte limestone

Muav limestone

Bright Angel shale

Dox formation

Shinumo quartzite

Hakatai shale

Diabase sill

Bass formation

Tapeats sandstone

Fossils

FOSSILS ARE THE REMAINS of plants and animals that have been preserved in rock. A fossil may be the preserved remains of an organism itself, an impression of it in rock, or preserved traces (known as trace fossils) left by an organism while it was alive, such as organic carbon outlines, fossilized footprints, or droppings. Most dead organisms soon rot away or are eaten by scavengers. For fossilization to occur, rapid burial by sediment is necessary. The organism decays, but the harder parts – bones, teeth, and shells, for example – may be preserved and hardened by minerals from the surrounding sediment. Fossilization may also occur even when the hard parts of an organism are dissolved away to leave an impression called a mould. The mould is filled by minerals, thereby creating a cast of the organism. The study of fossils (palaeontology) can not only show how living things have evolved, but can also help to reveal the Earth's geological history – for example, by aiding in the dating of rock strata.

PROCESS OF FOSSILIZATION

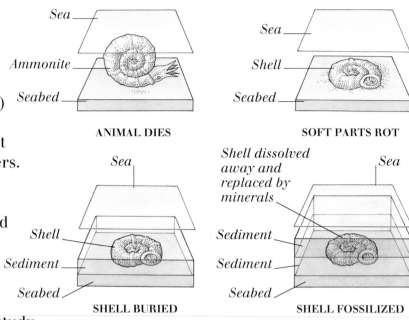

Sea
Ammonite
Seabed
ANIMAL DIES

Sea
Shell
Seabed
SOFT PARTS ROT

Sea
Shell
Sediment
Seabed
SHELL BURIED

Shell dissolved away and replaced by minerals
Sea
Sediment
Sediment
Seabed
SHELL FOSSILIZED

EXAMPLES OF FOSSILS

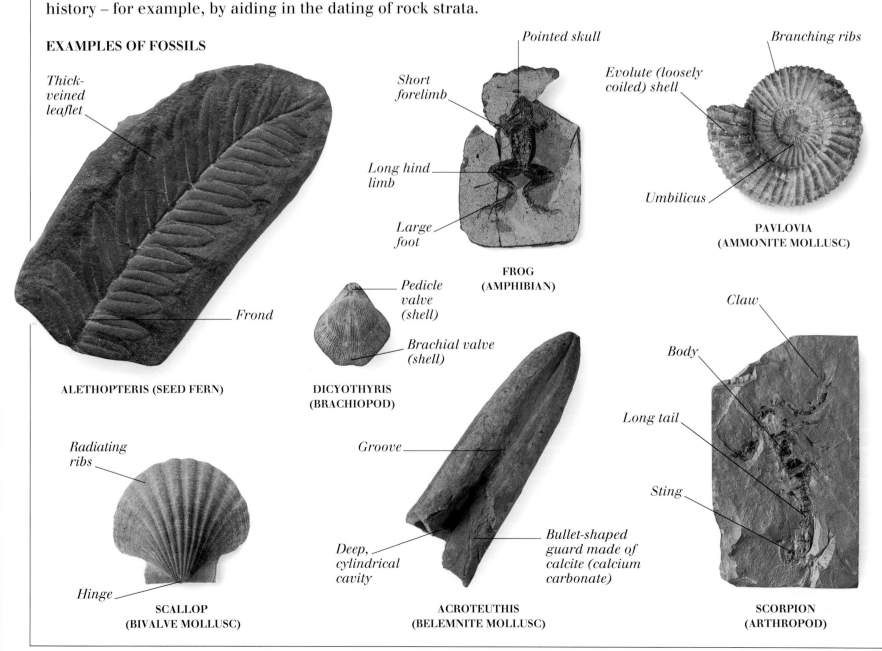

Thick-veined leaflet

Frond

ALETHOPTERIS (SEED FERN)

Radiating ribs

Hinge

SCALLOP (BIVALVE MOLLUSC)

Pointed skull

Short forelimb

Long hind limb

Large foot

FROG (AMPHIBIAN)

Pedicle valve (shell)

Brachial valve (shell)

DICYOTHYRIS (BRACHIOPOD)

Groove

Deep, cylindrical cavity

Bullet-shaped guard made of calcite (calcium carbonate)

ACROTEUTHIS (BELEMNITE MOLLUSC)

Evolute (loosely coiled) shell

Branching ribs

Umbilicus

PAVLOVIA (AMMONITE MOLLUSC)

Claw

Body

Long tail

Sting

SCORPION (ARTHROPOD)

THE FOSSIL RECORD

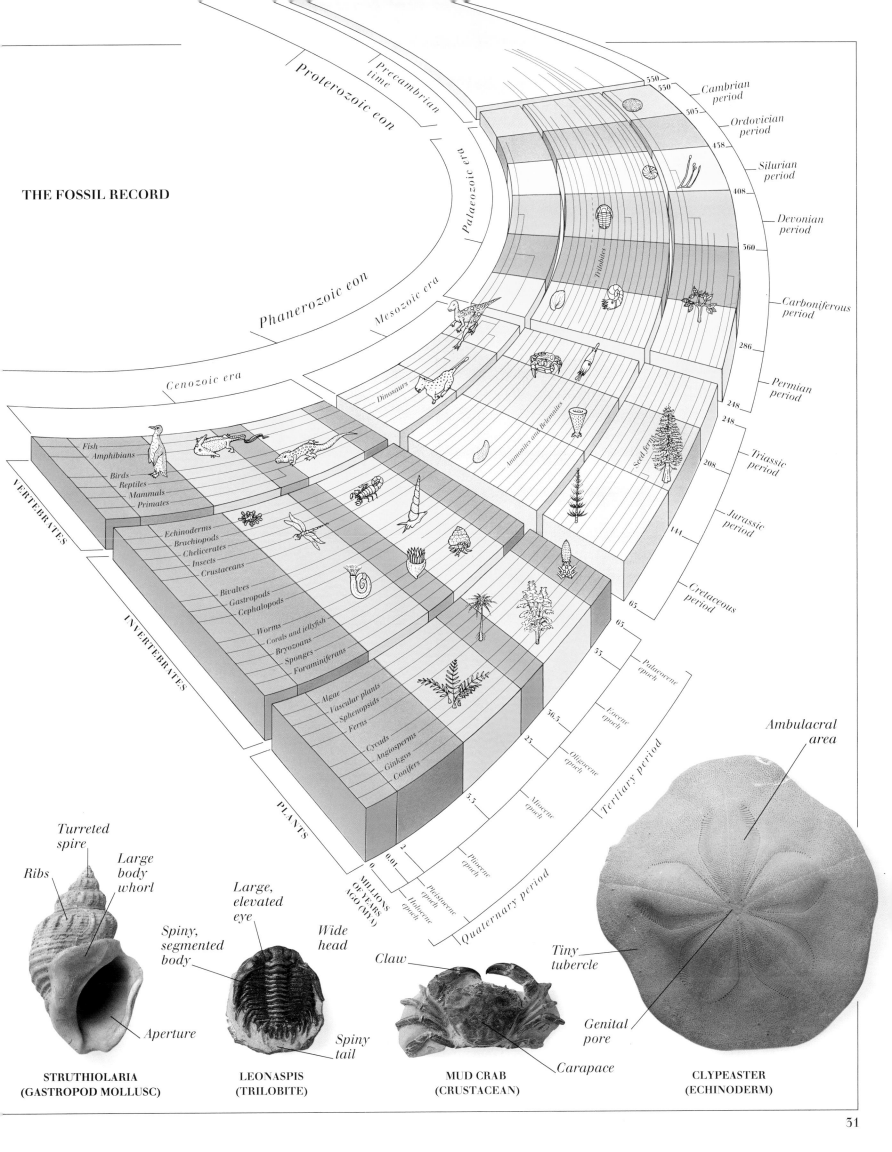

Precambrian time

Proterozoic eon

Phanerozoic eon

Palaeozoic era

Mesozoic era

Cenozoic era

550

Cambrian period

505

Ordovician period

438

Silurian period

408

Devonian period

360

Carboniferous period

286

Permian period

248

Triassic period

248

208

Jurassic period

144

Cretaceous period

65

65

55

Palaeocene epoch

36.5

Eocene epoch

25

Oligocene epoch

5.5

Miocene epoch

2

Pliocene epoch

0.01

Pleistocene epoch

0

Holocene epoch

Tertiary period

Quaternary period

MILLIONS OF YEARS AGO (MYA)

Trilobites

Dinosaurs

Ammonites and Belemnites

Seed fern

VERTEBRATES

Fish
Amphibians
Birds
Reptiles
Mammals
Primates

INVERTEBRATES

Echinoderms
Brachiopods
Chelicerates
Insects
Crustaceans
Bivalves
Gastropods
Cephalopods
Worms
Corals and jellyfish
Bryozoans
Sponges
Foraminiferans

PLANTS

Algae
Vascular plants
Sphenopsids
Ferns
Cycads
Angiosperms
Ginkgos
Conifers

Turreted spire

Ribs

Large body whorl

Aperture

**STRUTHIOLARIA
(GASTROPOD MOLLUSC)**

Large, elevated eye

Spiny, segmented body

Wide head

Spiny tail

**LEONASPIS
(TRILOBITE)**

Claw

Carapace

**MUD CRAB
(CRUSTACEAN)**

Ambulacral area

Tiny tubercle

Genital pore

**CLYPEASTER
(ECHINODERM)**

Mineral resources

MINERAL RESOURCES CAN BE DEFINED AS naturally occurring substances that can be extracted from the Earth and are useful as fuels and raw materials. Coal, oil, and gas – collectively called fossil fuels – are commonly included in this group, but are not strictly minerals, because they are of organic origin. Coal formation begins when vegetation is buried and partly decomposed to form peat. Overlying sediments compress the peat and transform it into lignite (soft brown coal). As the overlying sediments accumulate, increasing pressure and temperature eventually transform the lignite into bituminous and hard anthracite coals. Oil and gas are usually formed from organic matter that was deposited in marine sediments. Under the effects of heat and pressure, the compressed organic matter undergoes complex chemical changes to form oil and gas. The oil and gas percolate upwards through water-saturated, permeable rocks and they may rise to the Earth's surface or accumulate below an impermeable layer of rock that has been folded or faulted to form a trap – an anticline (upfold) trap, for example. Minerals are inorganic substances that may consist of a single chemical element, such as gold, silver, or copper, or combinations of elements (see pp. 22-23). Some minerals are concentrated in mineralization zones in rock associated with crustal movements or volcanic activity. Others may be found in sediments as placer deposits – accumulations of high-density minerals that have been weathered out of rocks, transported, and deposited (on river-beds, for example).

OIL RIG, NORTH SEA

Stalk

Leaf

PLANT MATTER

Decayed plant matter

About 60% carbon

PEAT

About 70% carbon

Crumbly texture

LIGNITE (BROWN COAL)

Powdery texture

About 80% carbon

BITUMINOUS COAL

About 95% carbon

Shiny surface

ANTHRACITE COAL

HOW COAL IS FORMED

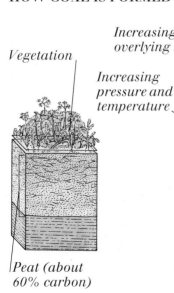
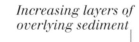
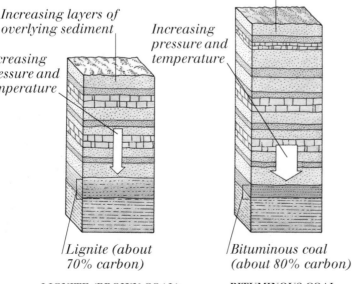

Increasing layers of overlying sediment

Increasing layers of overlying sediment

Vegetation

Increasing pressure and temperature

Increasing pressure and temperature

Peat (about 60% carbon)

Lignite (about 70% carbon)

Bituminous coal (about 80% carbon)

PEAT

LIGNITE (BROWN COAL)

BITUMINOUS COAL

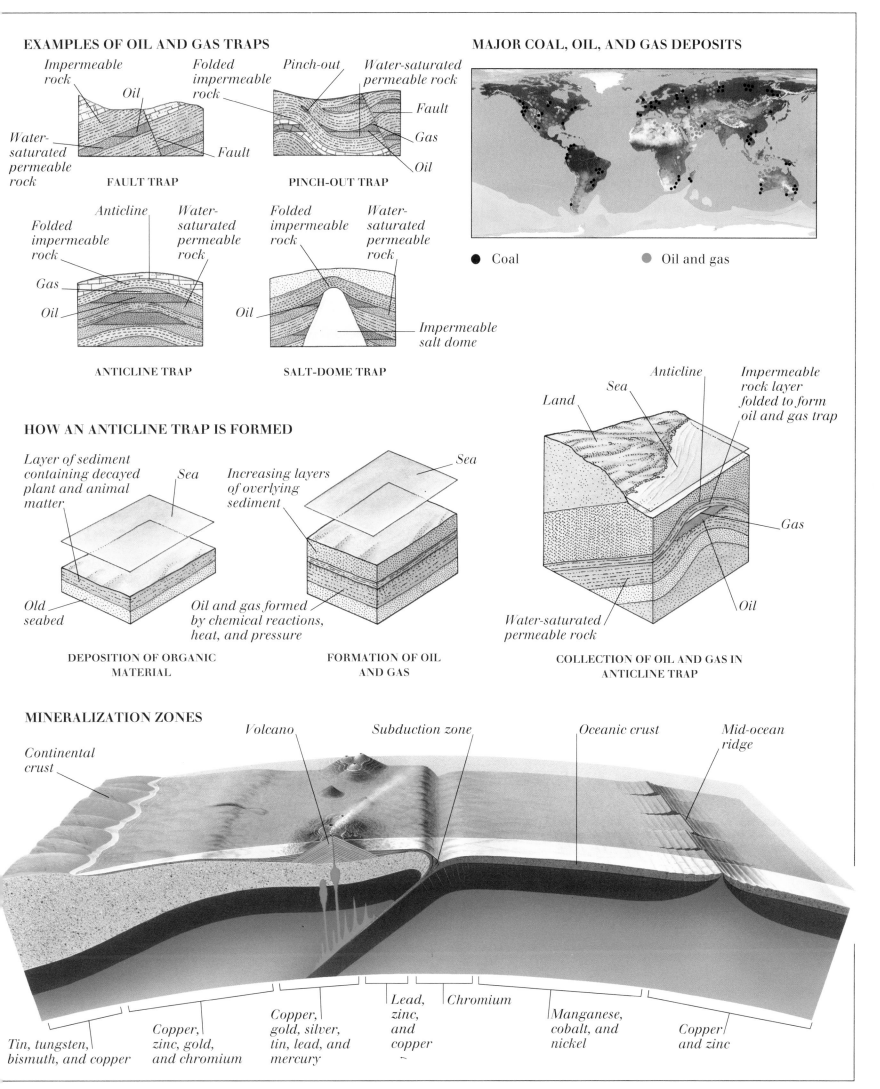

EXAMPLES OF OIL AND GAS TRAPS

Impermeable rock
Oil
Folded impermeable rock
Pinch-out
Water-saturated permeable rock
Water-saturated permeable rock
Fault
Fault
Gas
Oil

FAULT TRAP

PINCH-OUT TRAP

Anticline
Folded impermeable rock
Water-saturated permeable rock
Gas
Oil

Folded impermeable rock
Water-saturated permeable rock
Oil
Impermeable salt dome

ANTICLINE TRAP

SALT-DOME TRAP

MAJOR COAL, OIL, AND GAS DEPOSITS

● Coal   ● Oil and gas

HOW AN ANTICLINE TRAP IS FORMED

Layer of sediment containing decayed plant and animal matter
Sea
Old seabed

Increasing layers of overlying sediment
Sea
Oil and gas formed by chemical reactions, heat, and pressure

Land
Sea
Anticline
Impermeable rock layer folded to form oil and gas trap
Gas
Oil
Water-saturated permeable rock

DEPOSITION OF ORGANIC MATERIAL

FORMATION OF OIL AND GAS

COLLECTION OF OIL AND GAS IN ANTICLINE TRAP

MINERALIZATION ZONES

Continental crust
Volcano
Subduction zone
Oceanic crust
Mid-ocean ridge

Tin, tungsten, bismuth, and copper
Copper, zinc, gold, and chromium
Copper, gold, silver, tin, lead, and mercury
Lead, zinc, and copper
Chromium
Manganese, cobalt, and nickel
Copper and zinc

Weathering and erosion

WEATHERING IS THE BREAKING DOWN of rocks on the Earth's surface. There are two main types: physical (or mechanical) and chemical. Physical weathering may be caused by temperature changes, such as freezing and thawing, or by abrasion from material carried by winds, rivers, or glaciers. Rocks may also be broken down by the actions of animals and plants, such as the burrowing of animals and the growth of roots. Chemical weathering causes rocks to decompose by changing their chemical composition – for example, rainwater may dissolve certain minerals in a rock. Erosion is the wearing away and removal of land surfaces by water, wind, or ice. It is greatest in areas of little or no surface vegetation, such as deserts, where sand dunes may form.

FORMATION OF A HAMADA (ROCK PAVEMENT)

Wind blows away small particles

Larger particles aggregate

Hamada forms

FIRST STAGE **SECOND STAGE** **FINAL STAGE**

FEATURES OF WEATHERING AND EROSION

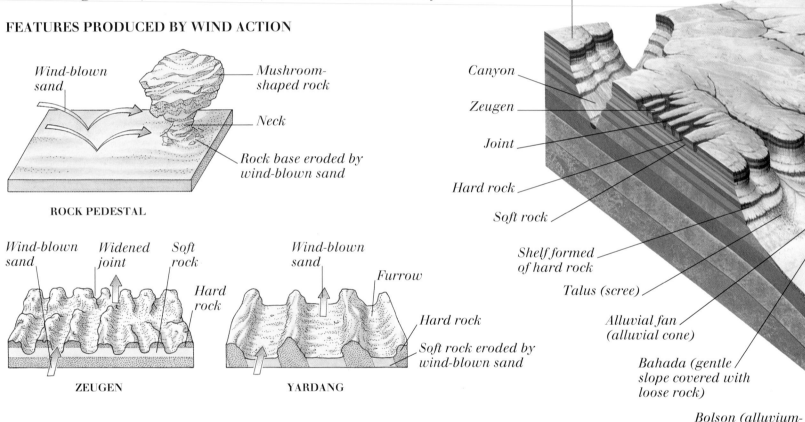

Mesa (flat-topped plateau)

Canyon

Zeugen

Joint

Hard rock

Soft rock

Shelf formed of hard rock

Talus (scree)

Alluvial fan (alluvial cone)

Bahada (gentle slope covered with loose rock)

Bolson (alluvium-filled basin)

FEATURES PRODUCED BY WIND ACTION

Wind-blown sand

Mushroom-shaped rock

Neck

Rock base eroded by wind-blown sand

ROCK PEDESTAL

Wind-blown sand *Widened joint* *Soft rock*

Hard rock

ZEUGEN

Wind-blown sand

Furrow

Hard rock

Soft rock eroded by wind-blown sand

YARDANG

EXAMPLES OF PHYSICAL WEATHERING PROCESSES

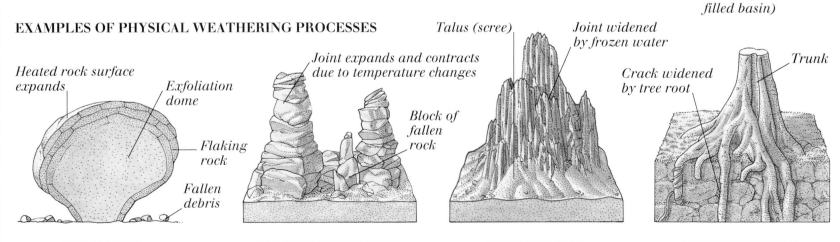

Heated rock surface expands

Exfoliation dome

Flaking rock

Fallen debris

EXFOLIATION (ONION-SKIN WEATHERING)

Joint expands and contracts due to temperature changes

Block of fallen rock

BLOCK DISINTEGRATION

Talus (scree)

Joint widened by frozen water

FROST WEDGING

Crack widened by tree root

Trunk

TREE ROOT ACTION

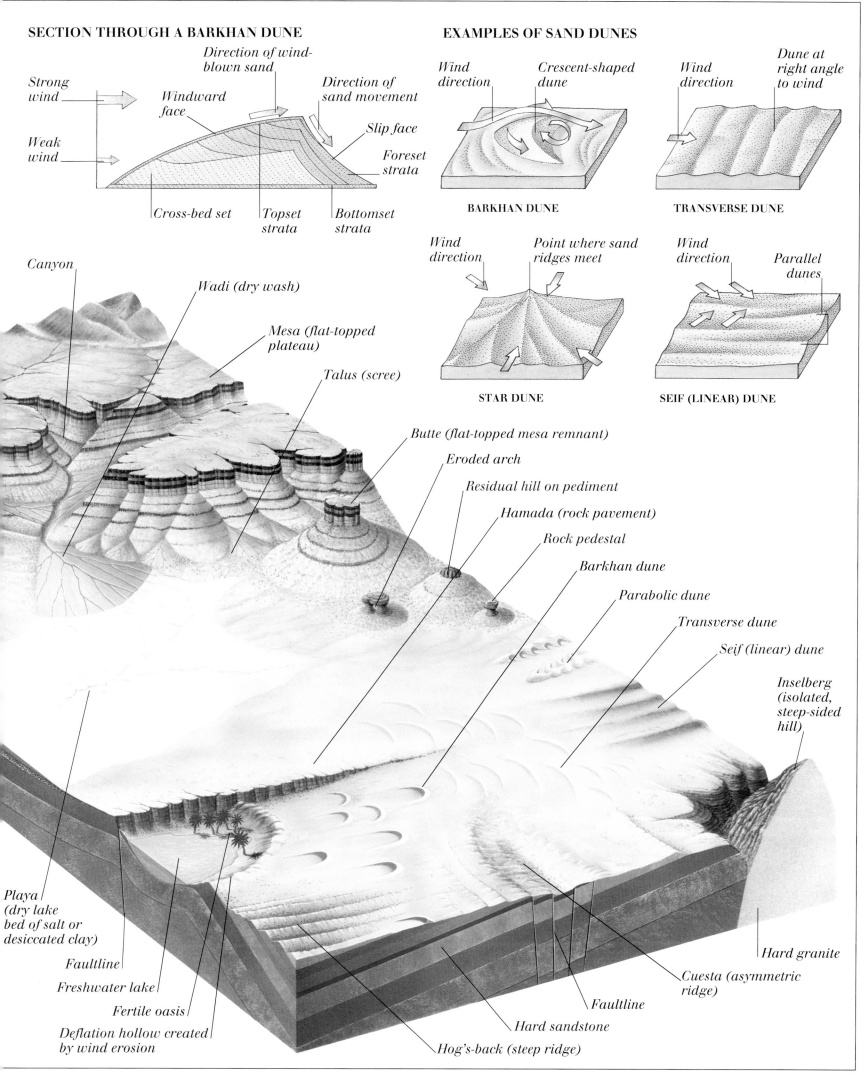

SECTION THROUGH A BARKHAN DUNE

Strong wind

Weak wind

Direction of wind-blown sand

Windward face

Direction of sand movement

Slip face

Foreset strata

Bottomset strata

Topset strata

Cross-bed set

EXAMPLES OF SAND DUNES

Wind direction

Crescent-shaped dune

BARKHAN DUNE

Wind direction

Dune at right angle to wind

TRANSVERSE DUNE

Wind direction

Point where sand ridges meet

STAR DUNE

Wind direction

Parallel dunes

SEIF (LINEAR) DUNE

Canyon

Wadi (dry wash)

Mesa (flat-topped plateau)

Talus (scree)

Butte (flat-topped mesa remnant)

Eroded arch

Residual hill on pediment

Hamada (rock pavement)

Rock pedestal

Barkhan dune

Parabolic dune

Transverse dune

Seif (linear) dune

Inselberg (isolated, steep-sided hill)

Playa (dry lake bed of salt or desiccated clay)

Faultline

Freshwater lake

Fertile oasis

Deflation hollow created by wind erosion

Hog's-back (steep ridge)

Hard sandstone

Faultline

Cuesta (asymmetric ridge)

Hard granite

Caves

CAVES COMMONLY FORM in areas of limestone, although on coastlines they also occur in other rocks. Limestone is made of calcite (calcium carbonate), which dissolves in the carbonic acid naturally present in rainwater, and in humic acids from the decay of vegetation. The acidic water trickles down through cracks and joints in the limestone and between rock layers, breaking up the surface terrain into clints (blocks of rock), separated by grikes (deep cracks), and punctuated by sink-holes (also called swallow-holes or potholes) into which surface streams may disappear. Underground, the acidic water dissolves the rock around crevices, opening up a network of passages and caves, which can become large caverns if the roofs collapse. Various features are formed when the dissolved calcite is redeposited; for example, it may be redeposited along an underground stream to form a gour (series of calcite ridges), or in caves and passages to form stalactites and stalagmites. Stalactites develop where calcite is left behind as water drips from the roof; where the drops land, stalagmites build up.

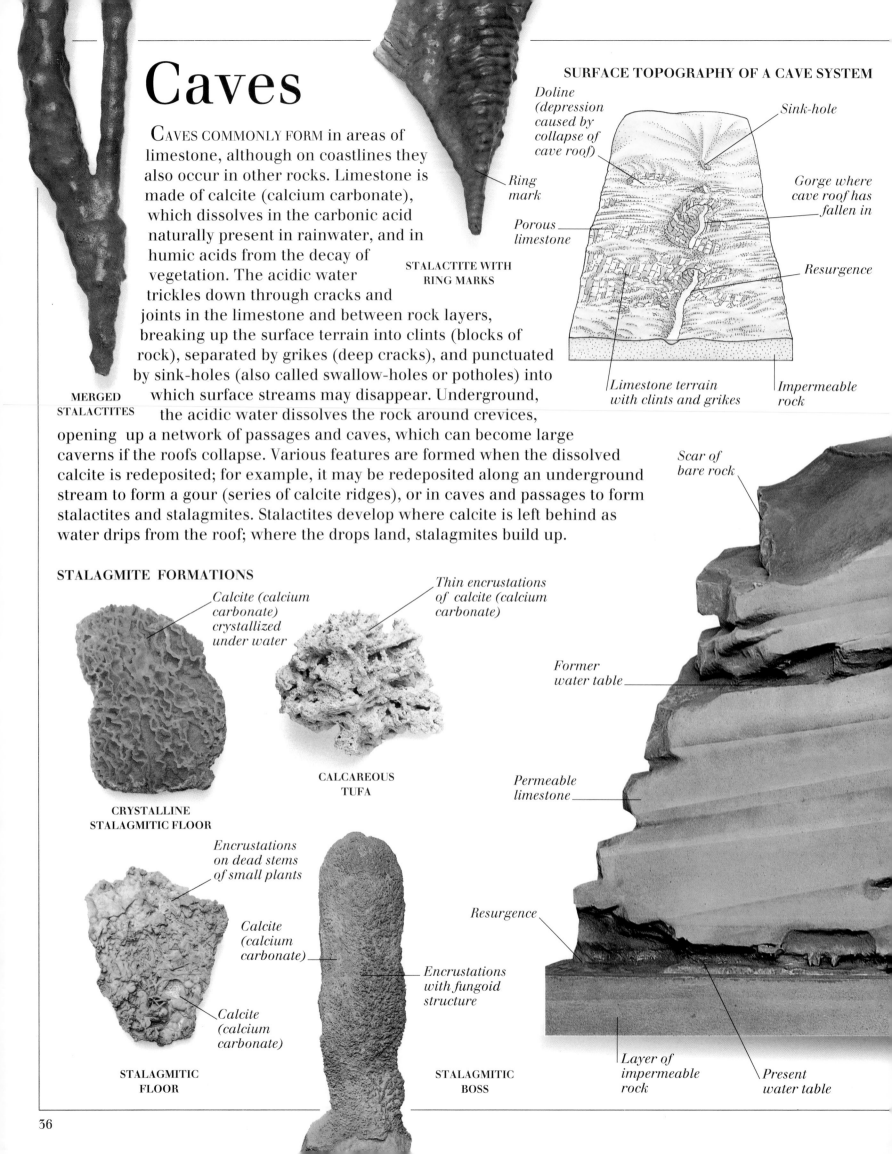

MERGED STALACTITES

STALACTITE WITH RING MARKS

Ring mark

SURFACE TOPOGRAPHY OF A CAVE SYSTEM

Doline (depression caused by collapse of cave roof)

Sink-hole

Gorge where cave roof has fallen in

Porous limestone

Resurgence

Limestone terrain with clints and grikes

Impermeable rock

STALAGMITE FORMATIONS

Calcite (calcium carbonate) crystallized under water

CRYSTALLINE STALAGMITIC FLOOR

Thin encrustations of calcite (calcium carbonate)

CALCAREOUS TUFA

Encrustations on dead stems of small plants

Calcite (calcium carbonate)

Calcite (calcium carbonate)

STALAGMITIC FLOOR

Calcite (calcium carbonate)

Encrustations with fungoid structure

STALAGMITIC BOSS

Scar of bare rock

Former water table

Permeable limestone

Resurgence

Layer of impermeable rock

Present water table

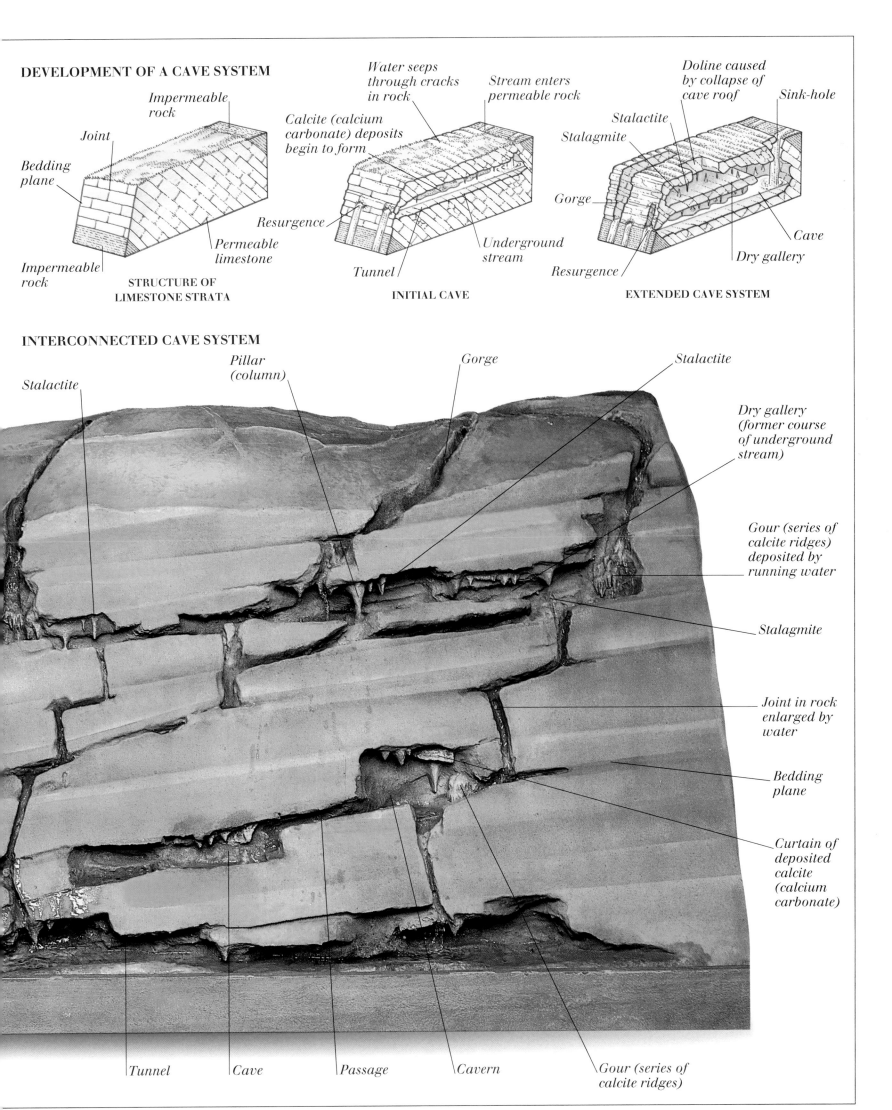

DEVELOPMENT OF A CAVE SYSTEM

STRUCTURE OF LIMESTONE STRATA

Impermeable rock

Joint

Bedding plane

Impermeable rock

Permeable limestone

INITIAL CAVE

Water seeps through cracks in rock

Stream enters permeable rock

Calcite (calcium carbonate) deposits begin to form

Resurgence

Tunnel

Underground stream

EXTENDED CAVE SYSTEM

Doline caused by collapse of cave roof

Sink-hole

Stalactite

Stalagmite

Gorge

Resurgence

Cave

Dry gallery

INTERCONNECTED CAVE SYSTEM

Stalactite

Pillar (column)

Gorge

Stalactite

Dry gallery (former course of underground stream)

Gour (series of calcite ridges) deposited by running water

Stalagmite

Joint in rock enlarged by water

Bedding plane

Curtain of deposited calcite (calcium carbonate)

Tunnel

Cave

Passage

Cavern

Gour (series of calcite ridges)

Glaciers

GLACIER BAY, ALASKA

A VALLEY GLACIER IS A LARGE MASS OF ICE that forms on land and moves slowly downhill under its own weight. It is formed from snow that collects in cirques (mountain hollows also known as corries) and compresses into ice as more and more snow accumulates. The cirque is deepened by frost wedging and abrasion (see pp. 34-35), and arêtes (sharp ridges) develop between adjacent cirques. Eventually, so much ice builds up that the glacier begins to move downhill. As the glacier moves it collects moraine (debris), which may range in size from particles of dust to large boulders. The rocks at the base of the glacier erode the glacial valley, giving it a U-shaped cross-section. Under the glacier, *roches moutonnées* (eroded outcrops of hard rock) and drumlins (rounded mounds of rock and clay) are left behind on the valley floor. The glacier ends at a terminus (the snout), where the ice melts as fast as it arrives. If the temperature increases, the ice melts faster than it arrives, and the glacier retreats. The retreating glacier leaves behind its moraine and also erratics (isolated single boulders). Glacial streams from the melting glacier deposit eskers and kames (ridges and mounds of sand and gravel), but carry away the finer sediment to form a stratified outwash plain. Lumps of ice carried on to this plain melt, creating holes called kettles.

VALLEY GLACIER

Lateral moraine
Meltwater pool
Medial moraine
Suspended erratic
Horn
Arête (ridge)
Englacial stream
Cave
Hanging valley
Melting glacier
Stream
Ice margin lake
Terminal moraine
Waterfall
Steep side of U-shaped valley
Braided stream
Boulder clay
Terminal lake
Meltwater stream
Roche moutonnée
Lake

Medial moraine
Suspended erratic
Snout
Push moraine
Terminal moraine
Roche moutonnée

POST-GLACIAL VALLEY

Collapsed sediment
Drumlin
Exposed valley floor
Roche moutonnée
Horn of mountain
Arête (ridge)
Kame terrace
Esker
Erratic
Lacustrine terrace
Post-glacial stream
Kame delta
Kettle
Terminal moraine
Kettle lake
Outwash terrace
Boulder clay
Kame
Roche moutonnée
Outwash fan
Steep side of U-shaped valley

FEATURES OF A GLACIER

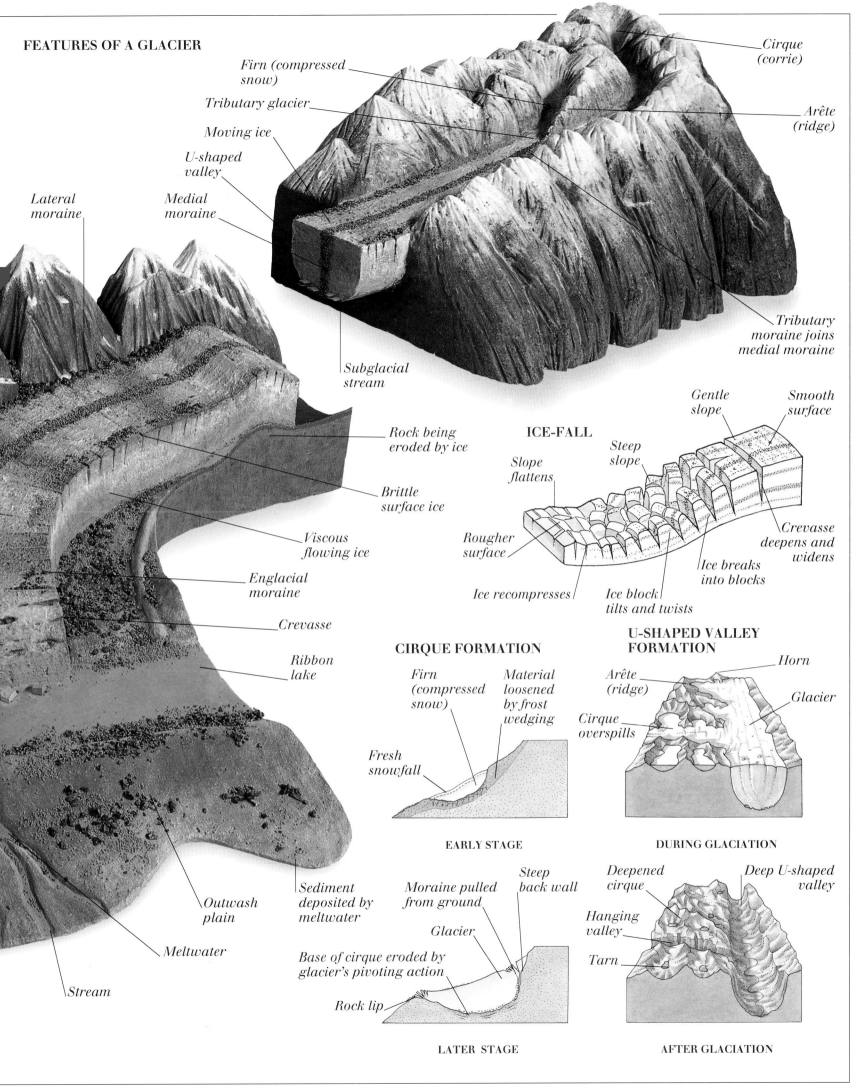

Firn (compressed snow)

Tributary glacier

Moving ice

U-shaped valley

Medial moraine

Lateral moraine

Cirque (corrie)

Arête (ridge)

Tributary moraine joins medial moraine

Subglacial stream

Rock being eroded by ice

Brittle surface ice

Viscous flowing ice

Englacial moraine

Crevasse

Ribbon lake

Sediment deposited by meltwater

Outwash plain

Meltwater

Stream

ICE-FALL

Gentle slope

Smooth surface

Steep slope

Slope flattens

Rougher surface

Ice recompresses

Ice block tilts and twists

Ice breaks into blocks

Crevasse deepens and widens

CIRQUE FORMATION

Firn (compressed snow)

Material loosened by frost wedging

Fresh snowfall

EARLY STAGE

Moraine pulled from ground

Steep back wall

Glacier

Base of cirque eroded by glacier's pivoting action

Rock lip

LATER STAGE

U-SHAPED VALLEY FORMATION

Arête (ridge)

Horn

Glacier

Cirque overspills

DURING GLACIATION

Deepened cirque

Deep U-shaped valley

Hanging valley

Tarn

AFTER GLACIATION

Rivers

RIVERS FORM PART of the water cycle – the continuous circulation of water between the land, sea, and atmosphere. The source of a river may be a mountain spring or lake, or a melting glacier. The course that the river subsequently takes depends on the slope of the terrain and on the rock types and formations over which it flows. In its early, upland stages, a river tumbles steeply over rocks and boulders and cuts a steep-sided V-shaped valley. Farther downstream, it flows smoothly over sediments and forms winding meanders, eroding sideways to create broad valleys and plains. On reaching the coast, the river may deposit sediment to form an estuary or delta (see pp. 42-43).

RIVER CAPTURE

Tributary erodes headwards

River

River

EARLY STAGE

Dry valley

River captured by tributary

River flow decreases

River flow increases

LATER STAGE

THE WATER CYCLE

Precipitation falls on high ground

Wind

Water vapour released into atmosphere by trees and other plants

Water carried downstream by river

Wind

Water vapour forms clouds

Water evaporates from sea

Water stored in sea

River flows into sea

Water seeps underground and flows to sea

Water evaporates from lake

Water seeps underground and flows to sea

Water seeps underground and flows to sea

SATELLITE IMAGE OF GANGES RIVER DELTA, BANGLADESH

River Ganges

Ganges delta

Infertile swampland

Distributary

Large volume of sediment

RIVER DRAINAGE PATTERNS

RADIAL

CENTRIPETAL

PARALLEL

DENDRITIC

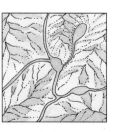

DERANGED

TRELLISED

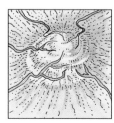

ANNULAR

RECTANGULAR

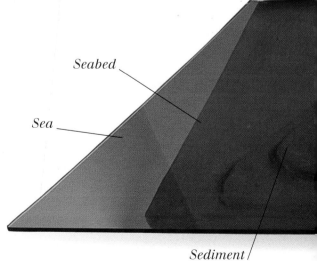

Seabed

Sea

Sediment layers

STAGES IN A RIVER'S DEVELOPMENT

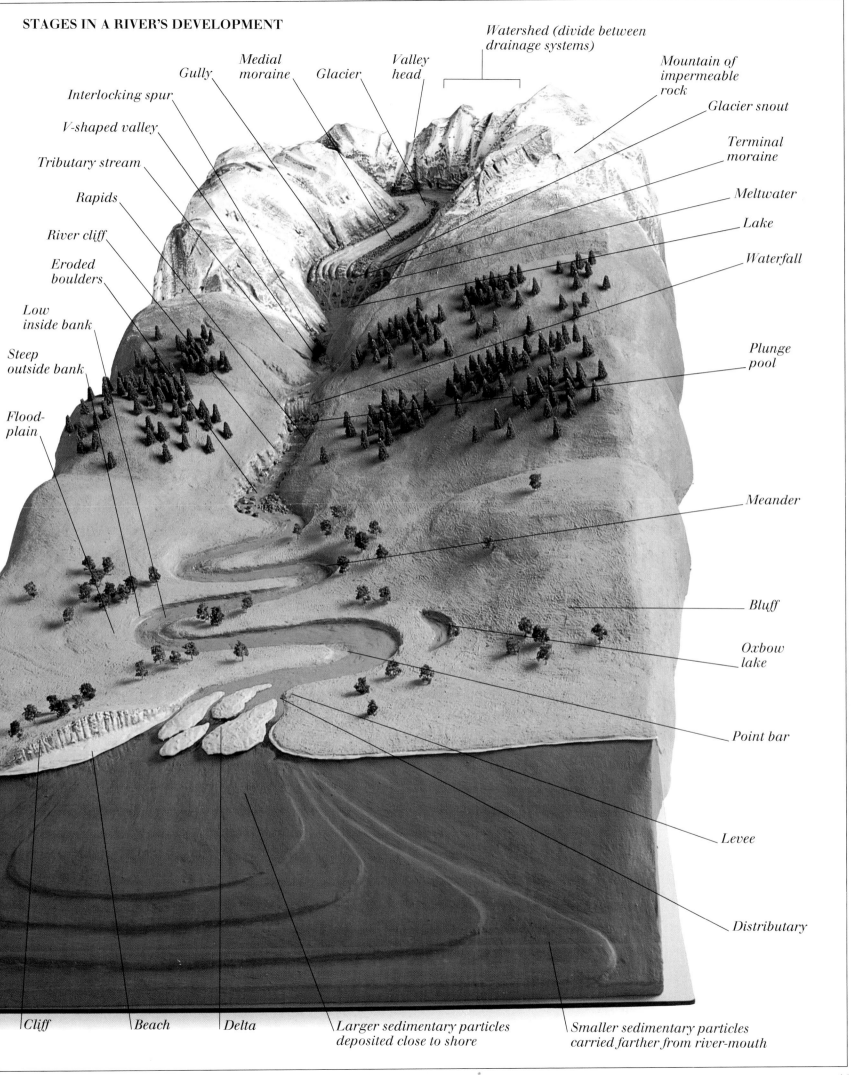

Watershed (divide between drainage systems)

Mountain of impermeable rock

Valley head

Glacier

Medial moraine

Gully

Interlocking spur

V-shaped valley

Tributary stream

Rapids

River cliff

Eroded boulders

Low inside bank

Steep outside bank

Flood-plain

Glacier snout

Terminal moraine

Meltwater

Lake

Waterfall

Plunge pool

Meander

Bluff

Oxbow lake

Point bar

Levee

Distributary

Cliff

Beach

Delta

Larger sedimentary particles deposited close to shore

Smaller sedimentary particles carried farther from river-mouth

41

River features

RIVERS ARE ONE OF THE MAJOR FORCES that shape the landscape. Near its source, a river is steep (see pp. 40-41). It erodes downwards, carving out V-shaped valleys and deep gorges. Waterfalls and rapids are formed where the river flows from hard rock to softer, more easily eroded rock. Farther downstream, meanders may form and there is greater sideways erosion, resulting in a broad river valley. The river sometimes erodes through the neck of a meander to form an oxbow lake. Sediment deposited on the valley floor by meandering rivers and during floods helps to create a flood-plain. Floods may also deposit sediment on the banks of the river to form levees. As a river spills into the sea or a lake, it deposits large amounts of sediment, and may form a delta. A delta is an area of sand-bars, swamps, and lagoons through which the river flows in several channels called distributaries – the Mississippi delta, for example. Often, a rise in sea level may have flooded the river-mouth to form a broad estuary, a tidal section where seawater mixes with fresh water.

HOW WATERFALLS AND RAPIDS ARE FORMED

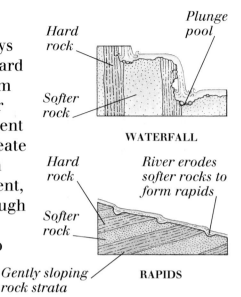

Hard rock

Plunge pool

Softer rock

WATERFALL

Hard rock

River erodes softer rocks to form rapids

Softer rock

Gently sloping rock strata

RAPIDS

A RIVER VALLEY DRAINAGE SYSTEM

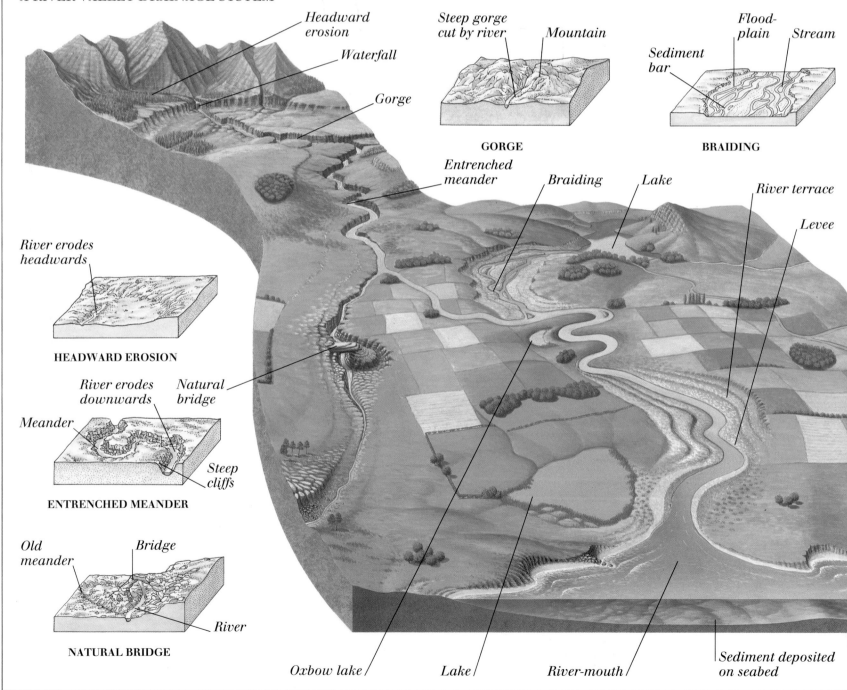

Headward erosion

Waterfall

Gorge

Steep gorge cut by river

Mountain

GORGE

Flood-plain

Stream

Sediment bar

BRAIDING

Entrenched meander

Braiding

Lake

River terrace

Levee

River erodes headwards

HEADWARD EROSION

River erodes downwards

Natural bridge

Meander

Steep cliffs

ENTRENCHED MEANDER

Old meander

Bridge

River

NATURAL BRIDGE

Oxbow lake

Lake

River-mouth

Sediment deposited on seabed

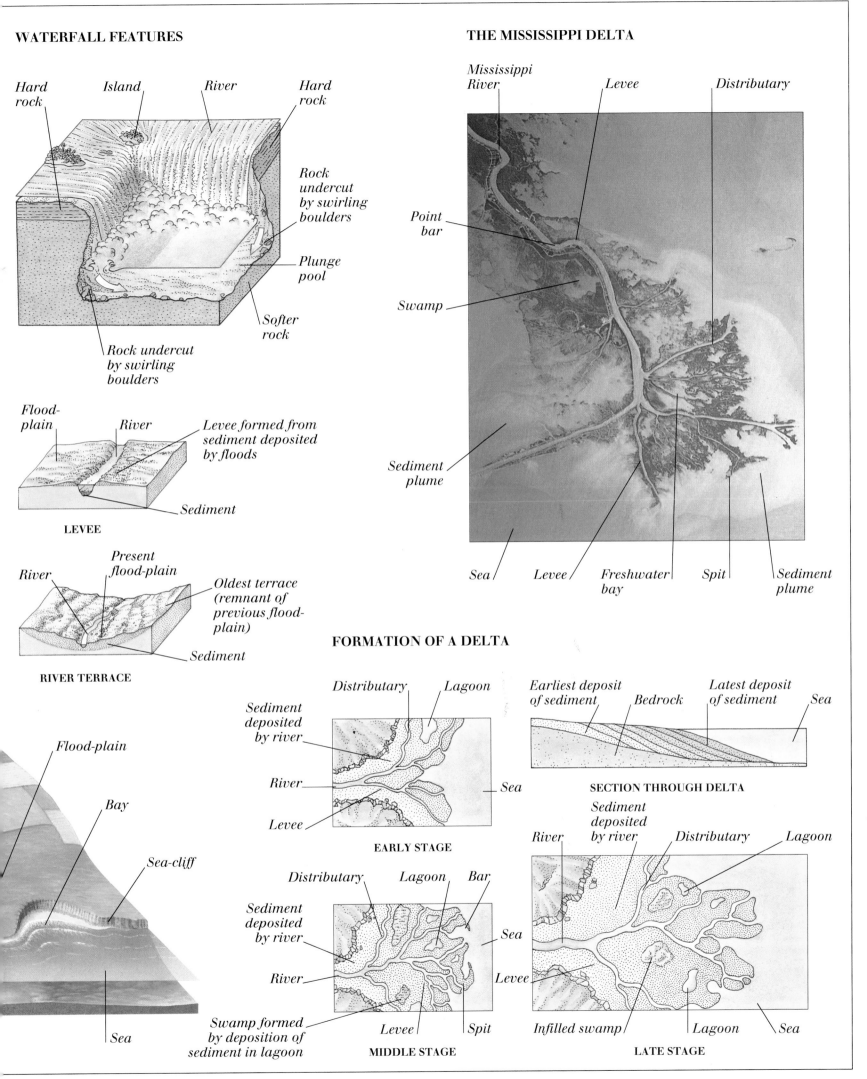

WATERFALL FEATURES

Hard rock

Island

River

Hard rock

Rock undercut by swirling boulders

Plunge pool

Softer rock

Rock undercut by swirling boulders

Flood-plain

River

Levee formed from sediment deposited by floods

Sediment

LEVEE

Present flood-plain

River

Oldest terrace (remnant of previous flood-plain)

Sediment

RIVER TERRACE

Flood-plain

Bay

Sea-cliff

Sea

THE MISSISSIPPI DELTA

Mississippi River

Levee

Distributary

Point bar

Swamp

Sediment plume

Sea

Levee

Freshwater bay

Spit

Sediment plume

FORMATION OF A DELTA

Distributary

Lagoon

Sediment deposited by river

River

Levee

Sea

EARLY STAGE

Earliest deposit of sediment

Bedrock

Latest deposit of sediment

Sea

SECTION THROUGH DELTA

Distributary

Lagoon

Bar

Sediment deposited by river

River

Levee

Spit

Sea

Swamp formed by deposition of sediment in lagoon

MIDDLE STAGE

Sediment deposited by river

River

Distributary

Lagoon

Levee

Infilled swamp

Lagoon

Sea

LATE STAGE

Lakes and groundwater

Natural lakes occur where a large quantity of water collects in a hollow in impermeable rock, or is prevented from draining away by a barrier, such as moraine (glacial deposits) or solidified lava. Lakes are often relatively short-lived landscape features, as they tend to become silted up by sediment from the streams and rivers that feed them. Some of the more long-lasting

LAKE BAIKAL, RUSSIA

lakes are found in deep rift valleys formed by vertical movements of the Earth's crust (see pp. 12-13) – for example, Lake Baikal in Russia, the world's largest freshwater lake, and the Dead Sea in the Middle East, one of the world's saltiest lakes. Where water is able to drain away, it sinks into the ground until it reaches a layer of impermeable rock, then accumulates in the permeable rock above it; this water-saturated permeable rock is called an aquifer. The saturated zone varies in depth according to seasonal and climatic changes. In wet conditions, the water

stored underground builds up, while in dry periods it becomes depleted. Where the upper edge of the saturated zone – the water table – meets the ground surface, water emerges as springs. In an artesian basin, where the aquifer is below an aquiclude (layer of impermeable rock), the water table throughout the basin is determined by its height at the rim. In the centre of such a basin, the water table is above ground level. The water in the basin is thus trapped below the water table and can rise under its own pressure along faultlines or well shafts.

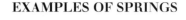

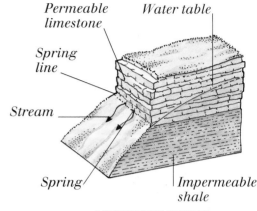

LIMESTONE SPRING

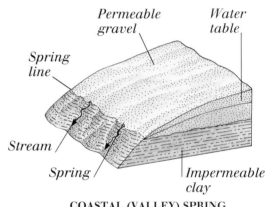

COASTAL (VALLEY) SPRING

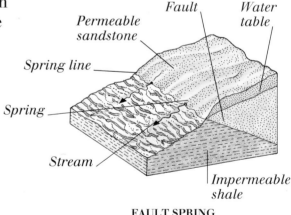

FAULT SPRING

STRUCTURE OF AN ARTESIAN BASIN

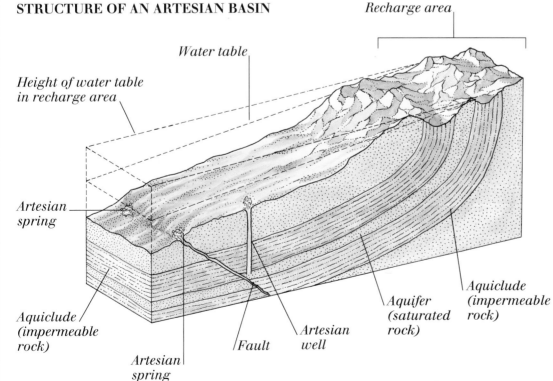

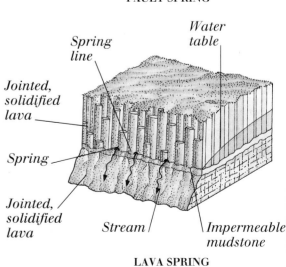

LAVA SPRING

FEATURES OF A GROUNDWATER SYSTEM

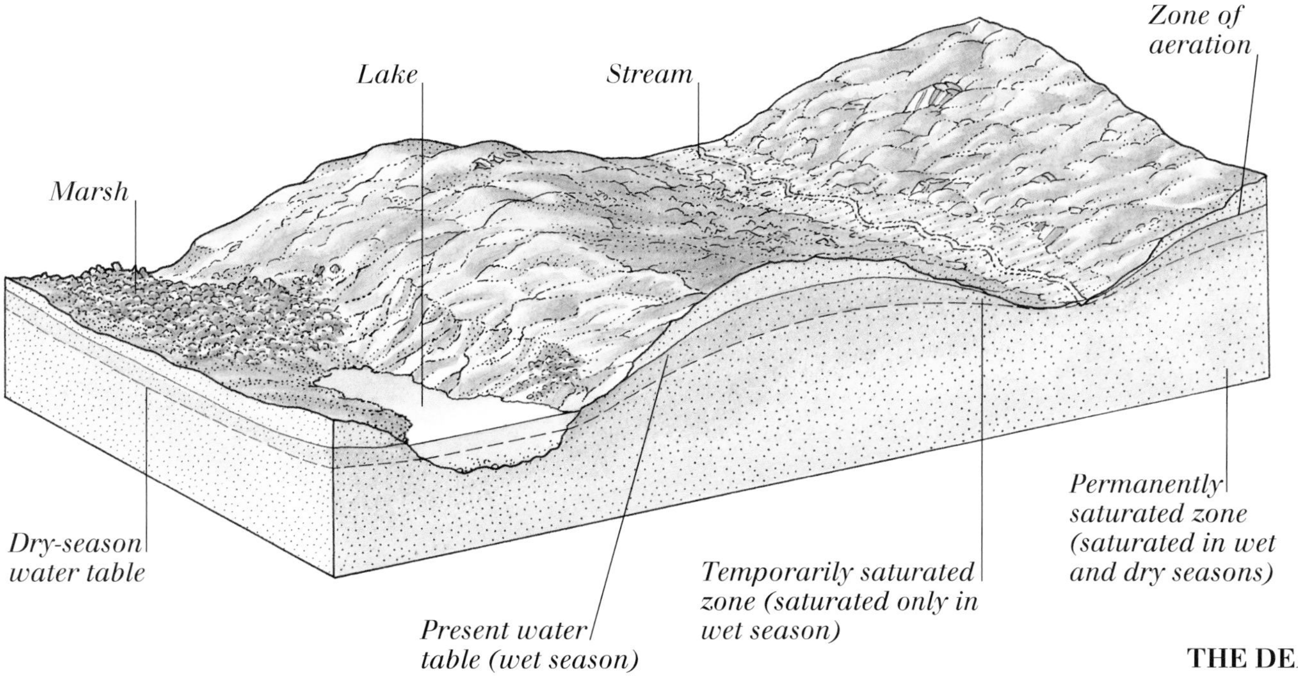

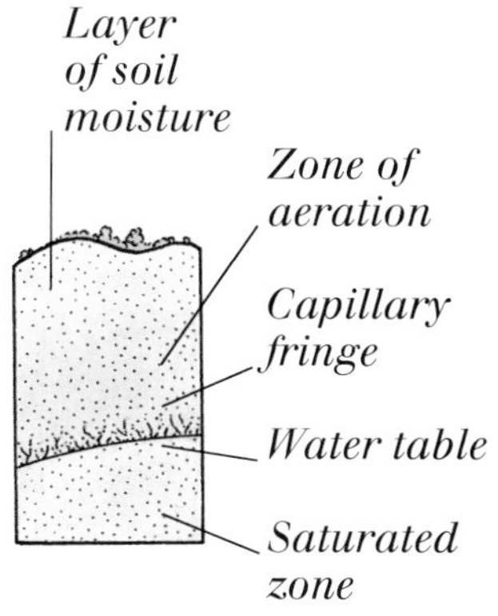

Marsh

Lake

Stream

Zone of aeration

Layer of soil moisture

Zone of aeration

Capillary fringe

Water table

Saturated zone

CLOSE-UP OF SURFACE LAYER

Dry-season water table

Present water table (wet season)

Temporarily saturated zone (saturated only in wet season)

Permanently saturated zone (saturated in wet and dry seasons)

EXAMPLES OF LAKES

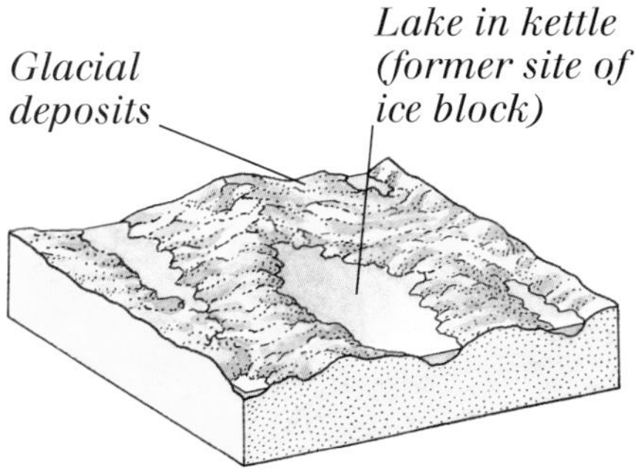

Glacial deposits

Lake in kettle (former site of ice block)

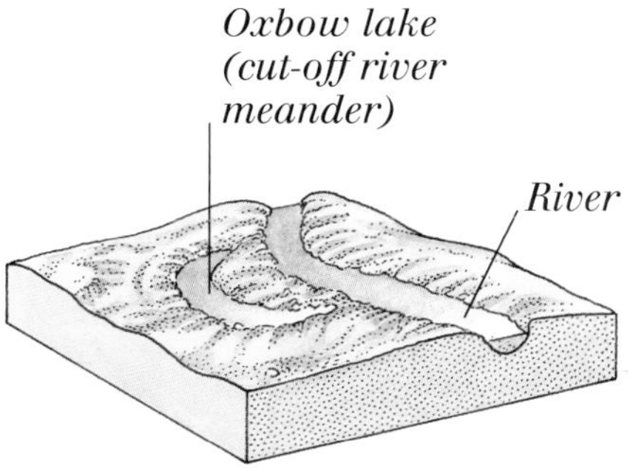

Oxbow lake (cut-off river meander)

River

KETTLE LAKE

OXBOW LAKE

Caldera (collapsed crater)

Volcanic lake

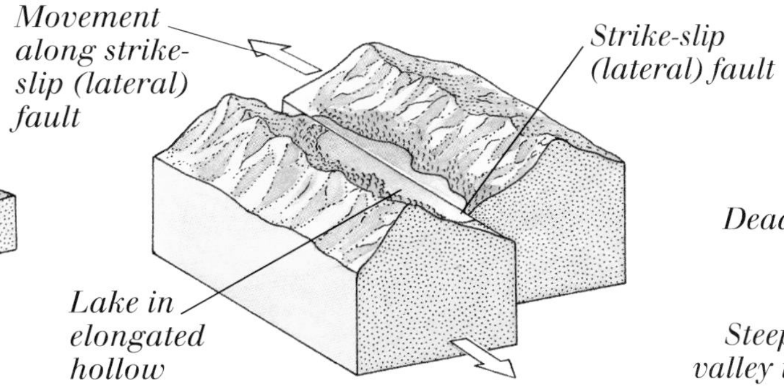

Movement along strike-slip (lateral) fault

Strike-slip (lateral) fault

Lake in elongated hollow

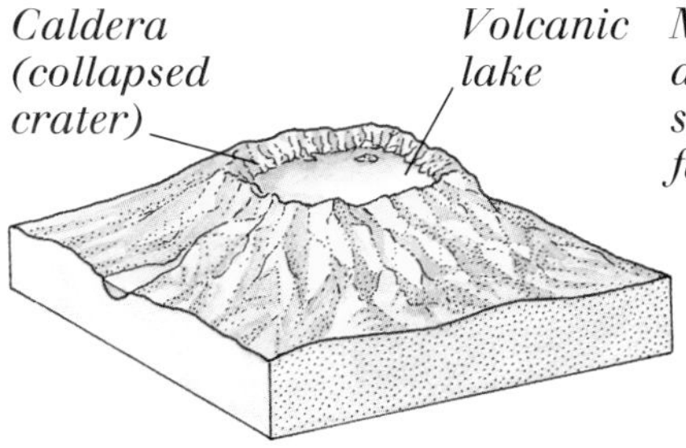

VOLCANIC LAKE

STRIKE-SLIP (LATERAL) FAULT LAKE

Rift valley

Steep back wall eroded by frost and ice

Moraine or rock lip damming lake

High valley walls

Sinking graben (block fault)

Tarn (circular mountain lake)

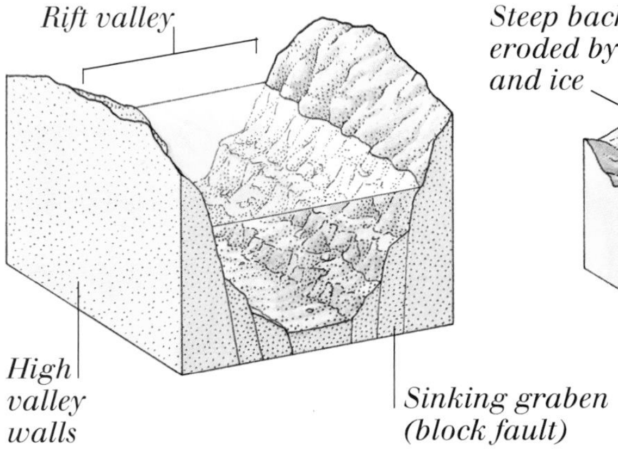

GRABEN (BLOCK-FAULT) LAKE

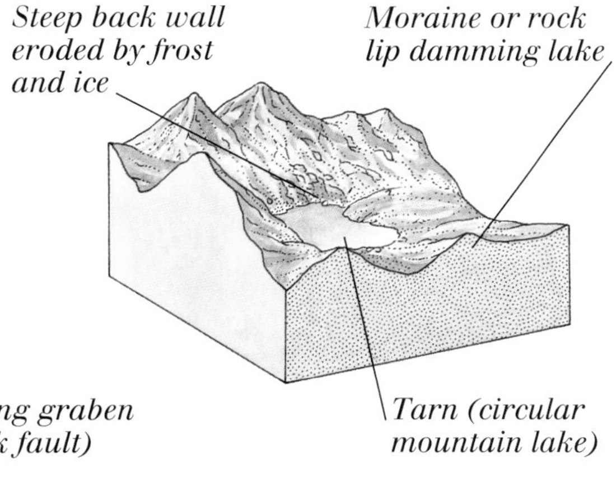

TARN

THE DEAD SEA, ISRAEL/JORDAN

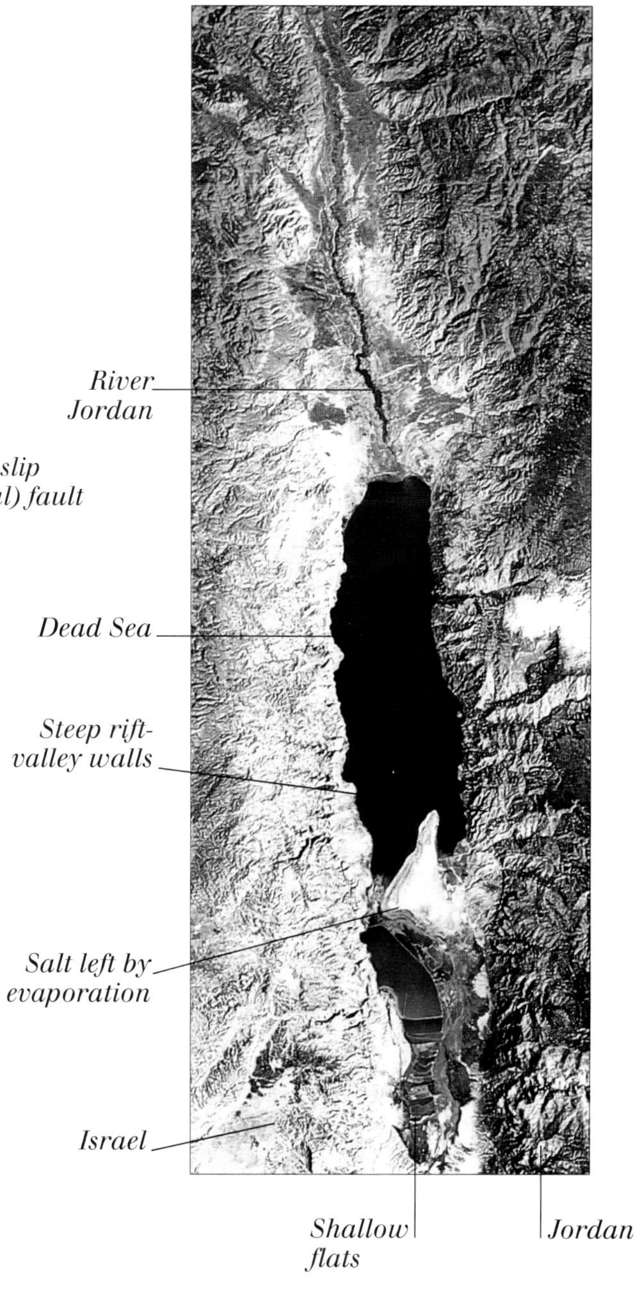

River Jordan

Dead Sea

Steep rift-valley walls

Salt left by evaporation

Israel

Shallow flats

Jordan

Coastlines

COASTLINES ARE AMONG THE MOST RAPIDLY changing landscape features. Some are eroded by waves, wind, and rain, causing cliffs to be undercut and caves to be hollowed out of solid rock. Others are built up by waves transporting sand and small rocks in a process known as longshore drift, and by rivers depositing sediment in deltas. Additional influences include the activities of living organisms such as coral, crustal movements, and sea-level variations due to climatic changes. Rising land or a drop in sea level creates an emergent coastline, with cliffs and beaches stranded above the new shoreline. Sinking land or a rise in sea level produces a drowned coastline, typified by fjords (submerged glacial valleys) or submerged river valleys.

FEATURES OF A SEA-CLIFF

Cliff-top
Cliff-face
High tide level
Low tide level
Offshore deposits
Wave-cut platform
Undercut area of cliff

FEATURES OF WAVES

Wave height
Crest
Wavelength
Trough
Shorter wavelength near beach
Circular orbit of water and suspended particles
Orbit deformed into ellipse as water gets shallower

LONGSHORE DRIFT

Pebble
Backwash
Movement of material along beach
Build-up of material against groyne
Beach
Groyne
Waves approaching shore at an oblique angle
Swash zone
Swash

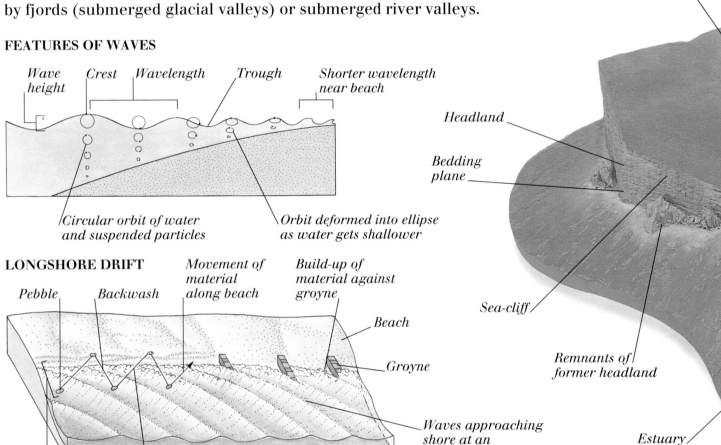

Mature river
Headland
Bedding plane
Sea-cliff
Remnants of former headland
Estuary

DEPOSITIONAL FEATURES OF COASTLINES

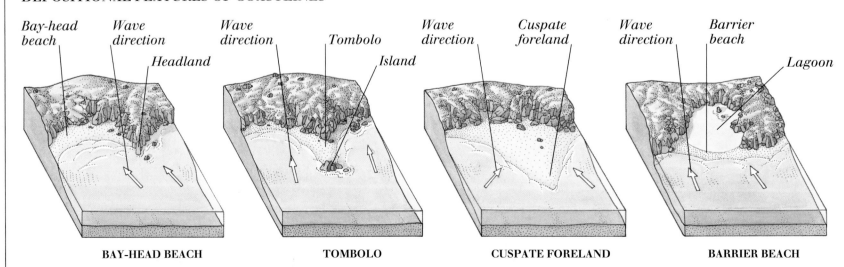

Bay-head beach
Wave direction
Headland

Wave direction
Tombolo
Island

Wave direction
Cuspate foreland

Wave direction
Barrier beach
Lagoon

BAY-HEAD BEACH

TOMBOLO

CUSPATE FORELAND

BARRIER BEACH

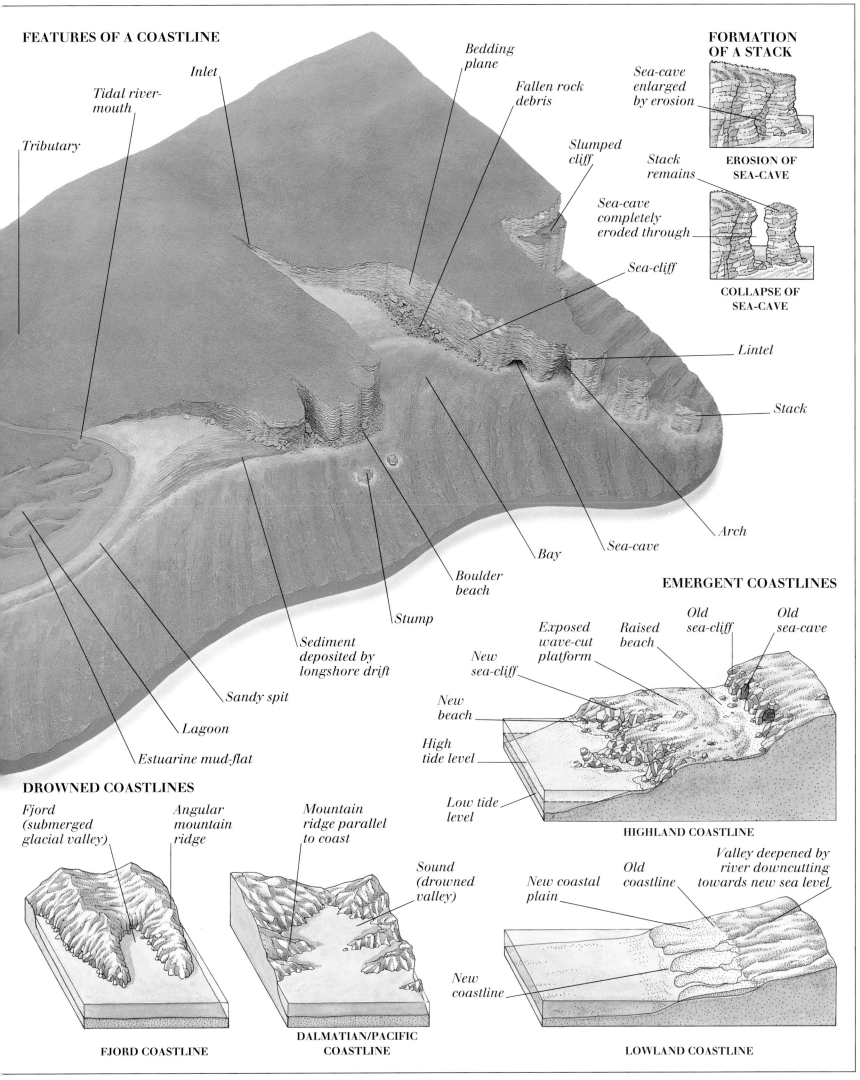

FEATURES OF A COASTLINE

Inlet

Tidal river-mouth

Tributary

Bedding plane

Fallen rock debris

Slumped cliff

Sea-cliff

Bay

Sea-cave

Arch

Boulder beach

Stump

Sediment deposited by longshore drift

Sandy spit

Lagoon

Estuarine mud-flat

FORMATION OF A STACK

Sea-cave enlarged by erosion

EROSION OF SEA-CAVE

Stack remains

Sea-cave completely eroded through

COLLAPSE OF SEA-CAVE

Lintel

Stack

EMERGENT COASTLINES

Exposed wave-cut platform

Raised beach

Old sea-cliff

Old sea-cave

New sea-cliff

New beach

High tide level

Low tide level

HIGHLAND COASTLINE

Valley deepened by river downcutting towards new sea level

Old coastline

New coastal plain

New coastline

LOWLAND COASTLINE

DROWNED COASTLINES

Fjord (submerged glacial valley)

Angular mountain ridge

Mountain ridge parallel to coast

Sound (drowned valley)

FJORD COASTLINE

DALMATIAN/PACIFIC COASTLINE

47

Oceans and seas

OCEANS AND SEAS COVER ABOUT 70 PER CENT of the Earth's surface and account for about 97 per cent of its total water. These oceans and seas play a crucial role in regulating temperature variations and determining climate. Their waters absorb heat from the Sun, especially in tropical regions, and the surface currents distribute it around the Earth, warming overlying air masses and neighbouring land in winter and cooling them in summer. The oceans are never still. Differences in temperature and salinity drive deep current systems, while surface currents are generated by winds blowing over the oceans. All currents are deflected – to the right in the Northern Hemisphere, to the left in the Southern Hemisphere – as a result of the Earth's rotation. This deflective factor is known as the Coriolis force. A current that begins on the surface is immediately deflected. This current in turn generates a current in the layer of water beneath, which is also deflected. As the movement is transmitted downwards, the deflections form an Ekman spiral. The waters of the oceans and seas are also moved by the constant ebb and flow of tides. These are caused by the gravitational pull of the Moon and Sun. The highest tides (Spring tides) occur at full and new Moon; the lowest tides (neap tides) occur at first and last quarter.

SURFACE CURRENTS

180° 160° 120° 80° 40° 0° GREENWICH MERIDIAN

Alaska Current
North Pacific Current
NORTH PACIFIC GYRE
North Equatorial Current
Equatorial Countercurrent
South Equatorial Current
SOUTH PACIFIC GYRE
Antarctic Circumpolar Current

East Greenland Current
North Atlantic Current
Florida Current
Gulf Stream
NORTH ATLANTIC GYRE
Canaries Current
North Equatorial Current
South Equatorial Current
Equatorial Countercurrent
Peru Current
Humboldt Current
Brazil Current
SOUTH ATLANTIC GYRE
Falkland Current

180° 160° 120° 80° 40° 0° GREENWICH MERIDIAN

OFFSHORE CURRENTS

SALT CONTENT OF SEAWATER

Potassium 1.1%
Magnesium 3.7%
Sodium 30.2%

Others 1.9%
Calcium 1.2%
Sulphate 7.6%
Chloride 54.3%

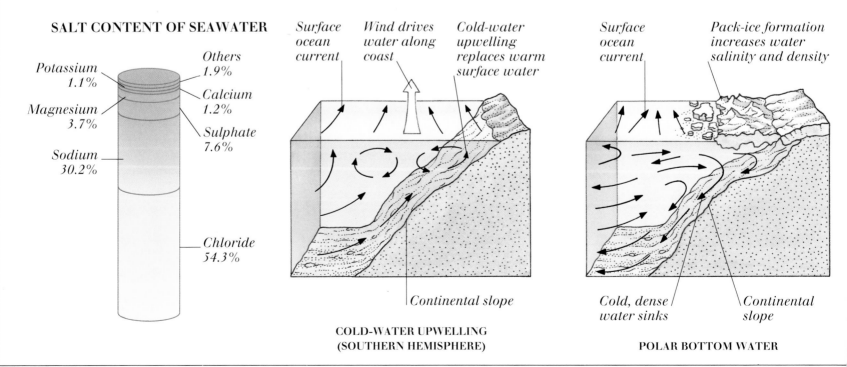

Surface ocean current
Wind drives water along coast
Cold-water upwelling replaces warm surface water

Continental slope

COLD-WATER UPWELLING (SOUTHERN HEMISPHERE)

Surface ocean current
Pack-ice formation increases water salinity and density

Cold, dense water sinks
Continental slope

POLAR BOTTOM WATER

48

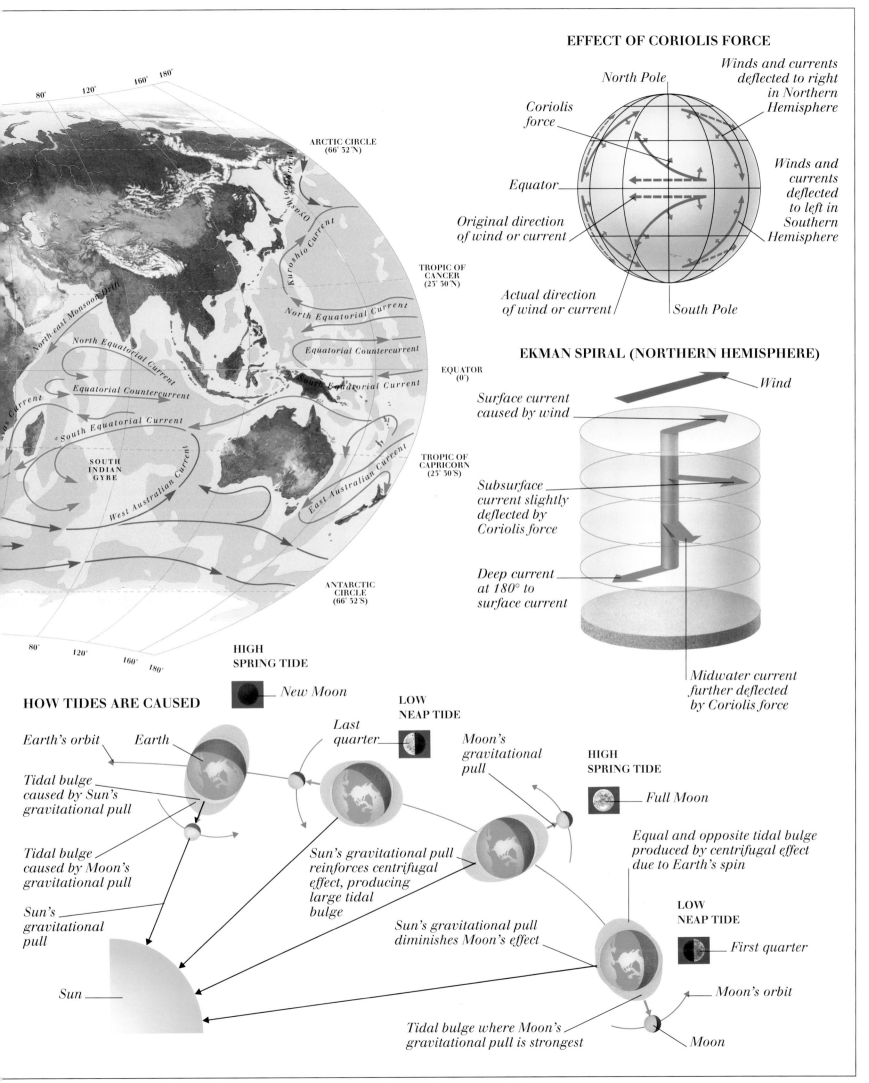

EFFECT OF CORIOLIS FORCE

North Pole

Coriolis force

Equator

Original direction of wind or current

Actual direction of wind or current

Winds and currents deflected to right in Northern Hemisphere

Winds and currents deflected to left in Southern Hemisphere

South Pole

ARCTIC CIRCLE
(66° 32´N)

TROPIC OF
CANCER
(23° 30´N)

EQUATOR
(0°)

TROPIC OF
CAPRICORN
(23° 30´S)

ANTARCTIC
CIRCLE
(66° 32´S)

Oyashio Current

Kuroshio Current

North-east Monsoon Drift

North Equatorial Current

North Equatorial Current

Equatorial Countercurrent

Equatorial Countercurrent

South Equatorial Current

South Equatorial Current

SOUTH
INDIAN
GYRE

West Australian Current

East Australian Current

EKMAN SPIRAL (NORTHERN HEMISPHERE)

Wind

Surface current caused by wind

Subsurface current slightly deflected by Coriolis force

Deep current at 180° to surface current

Midwater current further deflected by Coriolis force

HOW TIDES ARE CAUSED

HIGH
SPRING TIDE

New Moon

LOW
NEAP TIDE

Last quarter

Moon's gravitational pull

HIGH
SPRING TIDE

Full Moon

Earth's orbit

Earth

Tidal bulge caused by Sun's gravitational pull

Tidal bulge caused by Moon's gravitational pull

Sun's gravitational pull

Sun's gravitational pull reinforces centrifugal effect, producing large tidal bulge

Sun's gravitational pull diminishes Moon's effect

Equal and opposite tidal bulge produced by centrifugal effect due to Earth's spin

LOW
NEAP TIDE

First quarter

Moon's orbit

Sun

Tidal bulge where Moon's gravitational pull is strongest

Moon

The ocean floor

THE OCEAN FLOOR COMPRISES TWO SECTIONS: the continental shelf and slope, and the deep-ocean floor. The continental shelf and slope are part of the continental crust, but may extend far into the ocean. Sloping quite gently to a depth of about 140 metres, the continental shelf is covered in sandy deposits shaped by waves and tidal currents. At the edge of the continental shelf, the seabed slopes down to the abyssal plain, which lies at an average depth of about 3,800 metres. On this deep-ocean floor is a layer of sediment made up of clays, fine oozes formed from the remains of tiny sea creatures, and occasional mineral-rich deposits. Echo-sounding and remote sensing from satellites has revealed that the abyssal plain is divided by a system of mountain ranges, far bigger than any on land – the mid-ocean ridge. Here, magma (molten rock) wells up from the Earth's interior and solidifies, widening the ocean floor (see pp. 12-13). As the ocean floor spreads, volcanoes that have formed over hot spots in the crust move away from their magma source; they become extinct and are increasingly submerged and eroded. Volcanoes eroded below sea level remain as seamounts (underwater mountains). In warm waters, a volcano that projects above the ocean surface often acquires a fringing coral reef, which may develop into an atoll as the volcano becomes submerged.

CONTINENTAL-SHELF FLOOR

Bedrock exposed by tidal scour

Shoreline

Parallel strips of coarse material left by strong tidal currents

Sand deposited in wavy pattern by weaker currents

Irregular patches of fine sand deposited by weakest currents

FEATURES OF THE OCEAN FLOOR

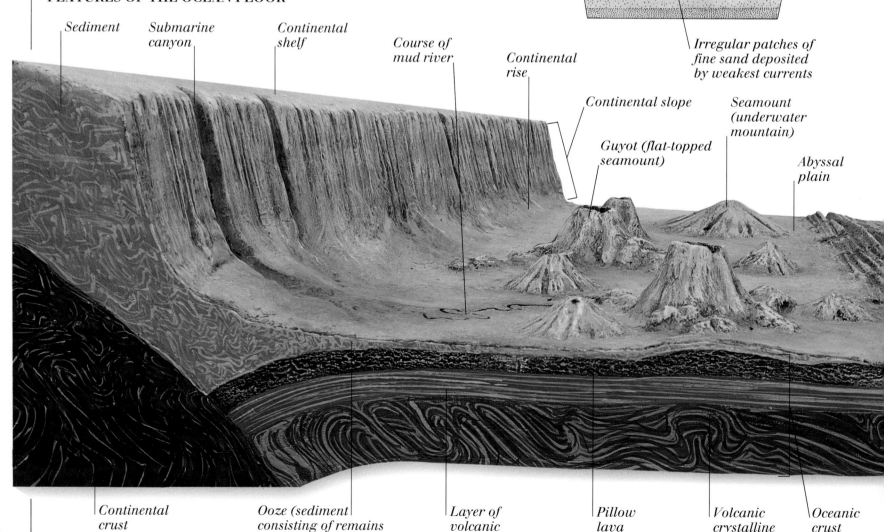

Sediment

Submarine canyon

Continental shelf

Course of mud river

Continental rise

Continental slope

Seamount (underwater mountain)

Guyot (flat-topped seamount)

Abyssal plain

Continental crust

Ooze (sediment consisting of remains of tiny sea creatures)

Layer of volcanic rock

Pillow lava

Volcanic crystalline rock

Oceanic crust

KEY

- Calcareous ooze
- Pelagic clay
- Glacial sediments
- Siliceous ooze
- Terrigenous sediments
- Continental margin sediments
- Metalliferous muds
- Major nodule fields

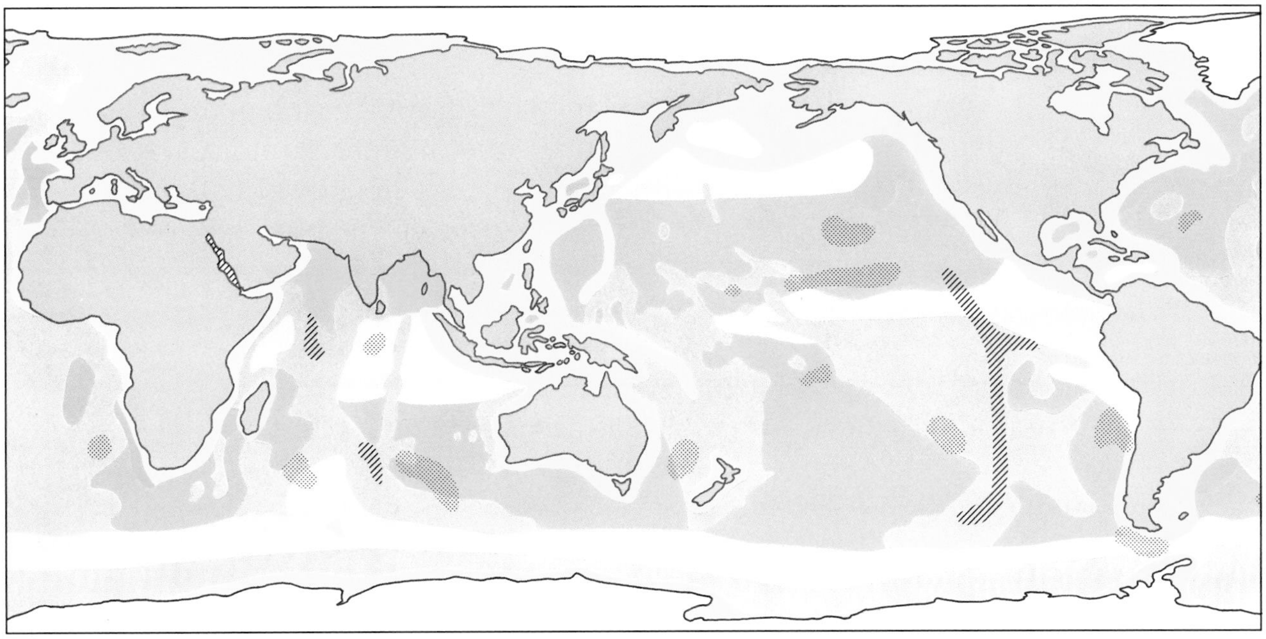

DEEP-OCEAN FLOOR SEDIMENTS

ECHO-SOUND PROFILE OF OCEAN FLOOR

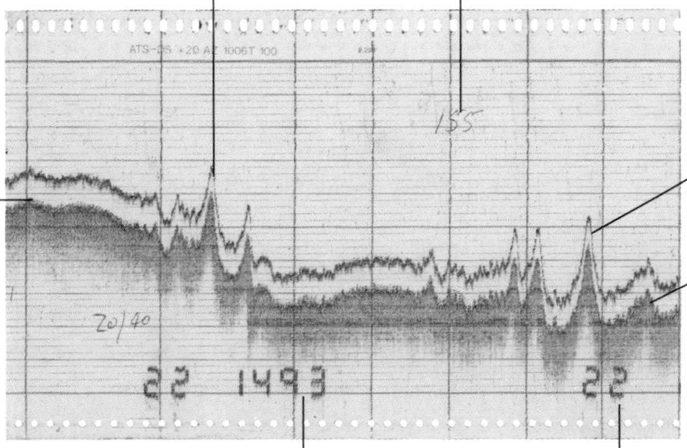

Sand wave

Event mark indicates synchronization of survey equipment

Sand wave

Seabed profile

Minor oscillations caused by ship's movement

Velocity of sound in water (1,493 m/sec)

Reference code

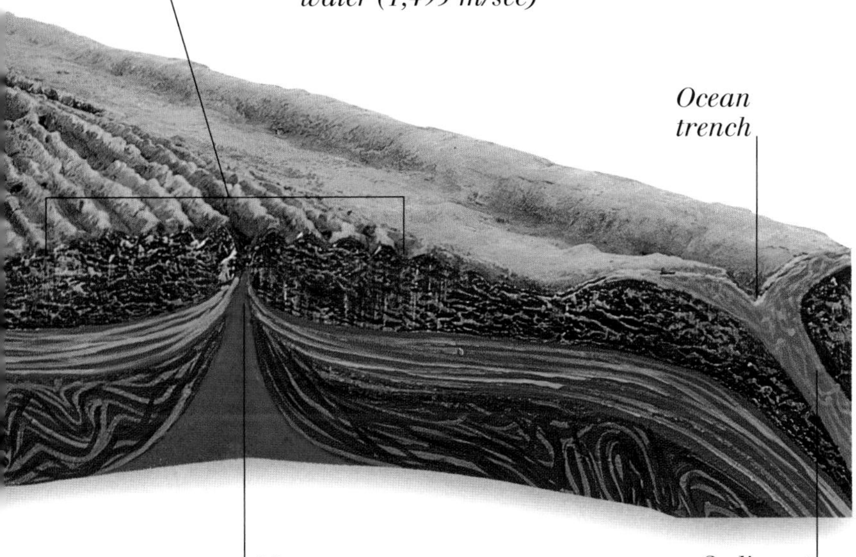

Mid-ocean ridge

Ocean trench

Magma (molten rock)

Sediment

DEVELOPMENT OF AN ATOLL

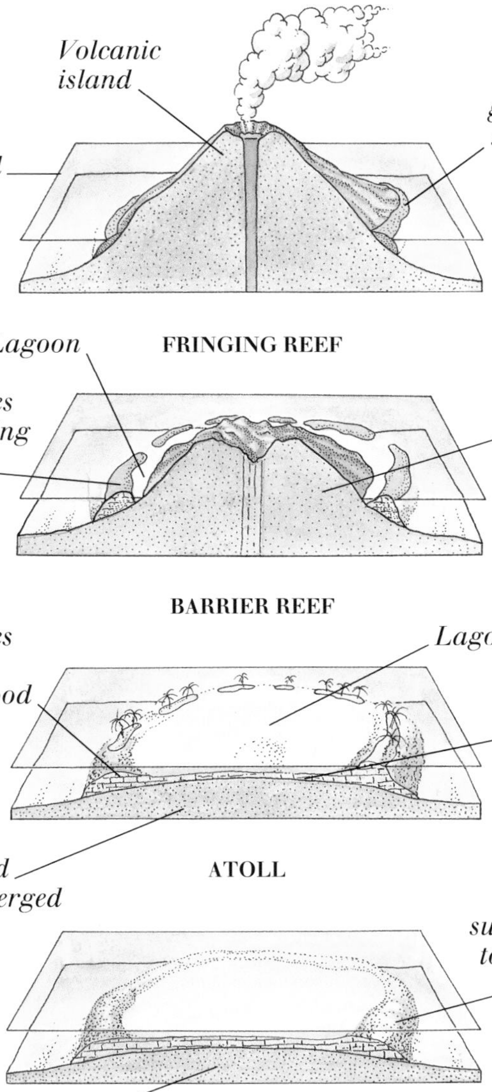

Volcanic island

Sea level

Coral grows on shoreline

FRINGING REEF

Lagoon

Eroded volcanic island subsides

Coral continues to grow, forming barrier reef

BARRIER REEF

Coral continues to grow where waves bring food

Lagoon

Dead coral

Volcanic island becomes submerged

ATOLL

Coral submerged too deeply to grow

Volcanic island is submerged further

SUBMERGED ATOLL

The atmosphere

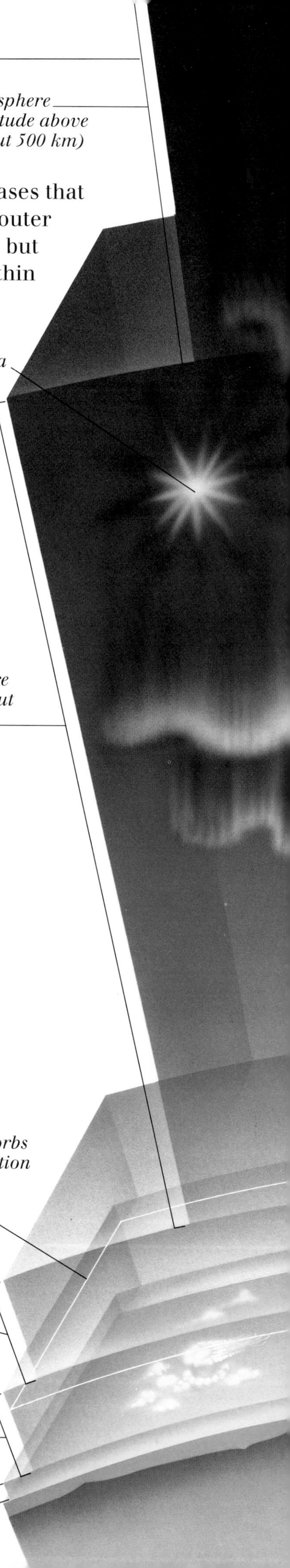

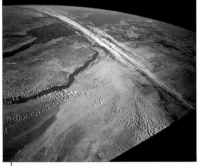

JET STREAM

THE EARTH IS SURROUNDED BY ITS ATMOSPHERE, a blanket of gases that enables life to exist on the planet. This layer has no definite outer edge, gradually becoming thinner until it merges into space, but over 80 per cent of atmospheric gases are held by gravity within about 20 kilometres of the Earth's surface. The atmosphere blocks out much harmful ultraviolet solar radiation, and insulates the Earth against extremes of temperature by limiting both incoming solar radiation and the escape of re-radiated heat into space. This natural balance may be distorted by the greenhouse effect, as gases such as carbon dioxide have built up in the atmosphere, trapping more heat. Close to the Earth's surface, differences in air temperature and pressure cause air to circulate between the equator and poles. This circulation, together with the Coriolis force, gives rise to the prevailing surface winds and the high-level jet streams.

ATMOSPHERIC CIRCULATION AND WINDS

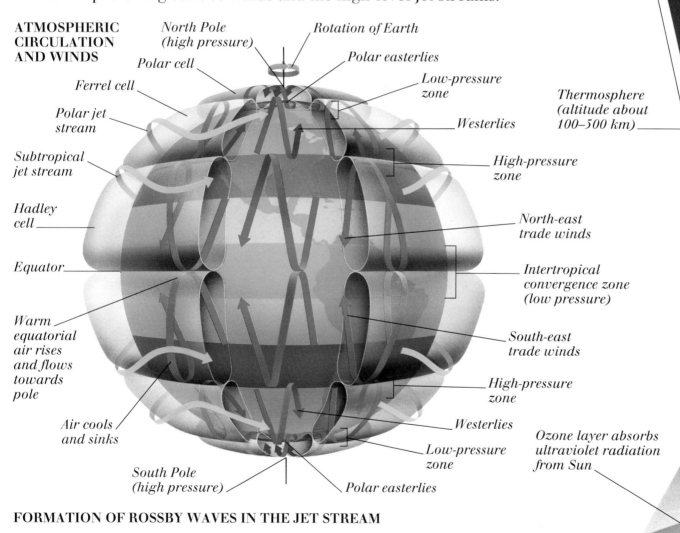

- Exosphere (altitude above about 500 km)
- Corona
- Thermosphere (altitude about 100–500 km)
- Ozone layer absorbs ultraviolet radiation from Sun
- Mesosphere (altitude about 50–100 km)
- Stratosphere (altitude about 10–50 km)
- Troposphere (altitude up to about 10 km)

Labels on globe diagram:
- North Pole (high pressure)
- Rotation of Earth
- Polar easterlies
- Polar cell
- Low-pressure zone
- Ferrel cell
- Westerlies
- Polar jet stream
- High-pressure zone
- Subtropical jet stream
- Hadley cell
- North-east trade winds
- Equator
- Intertropical convergence zone (low pressure)
- Warm equatorial air rises and flows towards pole
- South-east trade winds
- High-pressure zone
- Air cools and sinks
- Westerlies
- Low-pressure zone
- South Pole (high pressure)
- Polar easterlies

FORMATION OF ROSSBY WAVES IN THE JET STREAM

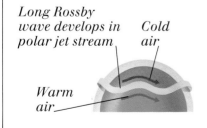

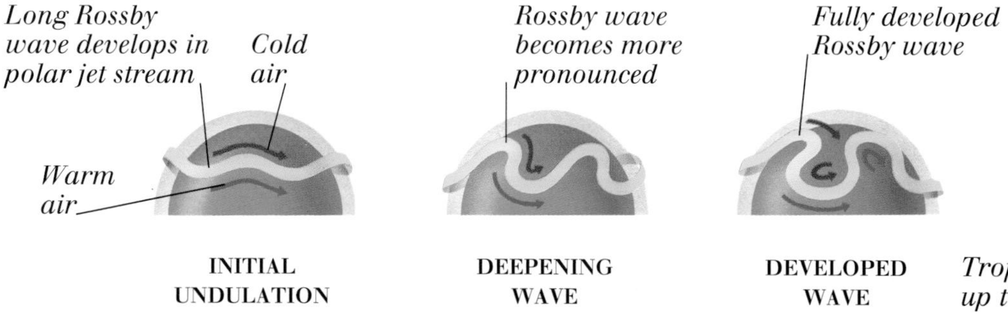

- Long Rossby wave develops in polar jet stream
- Cold air
- Rossby wave becomes more pronounced
- Fully developed Rossby wave
- Warm air

INITIAL UNDULATION **DEEPENING WAVE** **DEVELOPED WAVE**

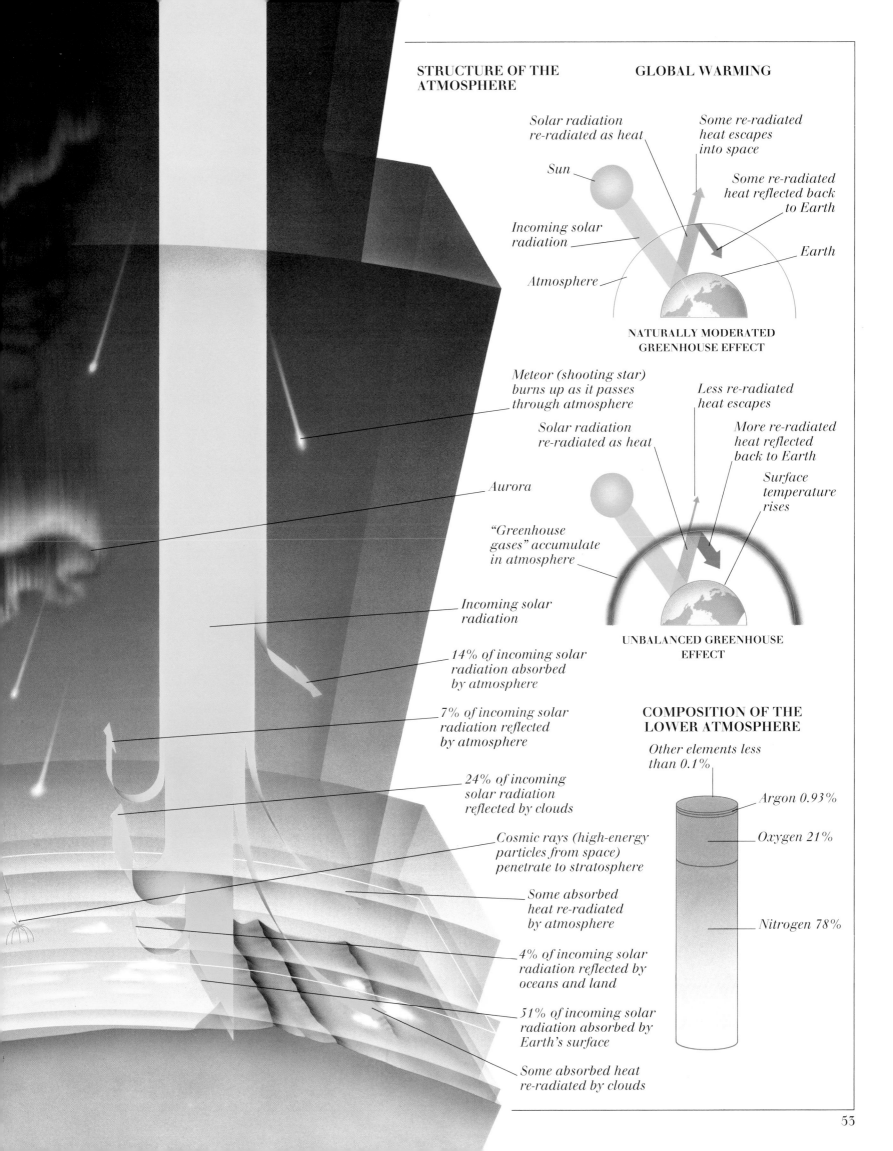

STRUCTURE OF THE
ATMOSPHERE

GLOBAL WARMING

Solar radiation
re-radiated as heat

Some re-radiated
heat escapes
into space

Sun

Some re-radiated
heat reflected back
to Earth

Incoming solar
radiation

Earth

Atmosphere

NATURALLY MODERATED
GREENHOUSE EFFECT

Meteor (shooting star)
burns up as it passes
through atmosphere

Less re-radiated
heat escapes

Solar radiation
re-radiated as heat

More re-radiated
heat reflected
back to Earth

Aurora

Surface
temperature
rises

"Greenhouse
gases" accumulate
in atmosphere

Incoming solar
radiation

UNBALANCED GREENHOUSE
EFFECT

14% of incoming solar
radiation absorbed
by atmosphere

7% of incoming solar
radiation reflected
by atmosphere

COMPOSITION OF THE
LOWER ATMOSPHERE

24% of incoming
solar radiation
reflected by clouds

Other elements less
than 0.1%

Argon 0.93%

Cosmic rays (high-energy
particles from space)
penetrate to stratosphere

Oxygen 21%

Some absorbed
heat re-radiated
by atmosphere

4% of incoming solar
radiation reflected by
oceans and land

Nitrogen 78%

51% of incoming solar
radiation absorbed by
Earth's surface

Some absorbed heat
re-radiated by clouds

Weather

WEATHER IS DEFINED AS THE ATMOSPHERIC CONDITIONS at a particular time and place; climate is the average weather conditions for a given region over time. Weather is assessed in terms of temperature, wind, cloud cover, and precipitation, such as rain or snow. Fine weather is associated with high-pressure areas, where air is sinking. Cloudy, wet, changeable weather is common in low-pressure zones with rising, unstable air. Such conditions occur at temperate latitudes, where warm air meets cool air along the polar fronts. Here, spiralling low-pressure cells known as depressions (mid-latitude cyclones) often form. A depression usually contains a sector of warmer air, beginning at a warm front and ending at a cold front. If the two fronts merge, forming an occluded front, the warm air is pushed upwards. An extreme form of low-pressure cell is a hurricane (also called a typhoon or tropical cyclone), which brings torrential rain and exceptionally strong winds.

TYPES OF CLOUD

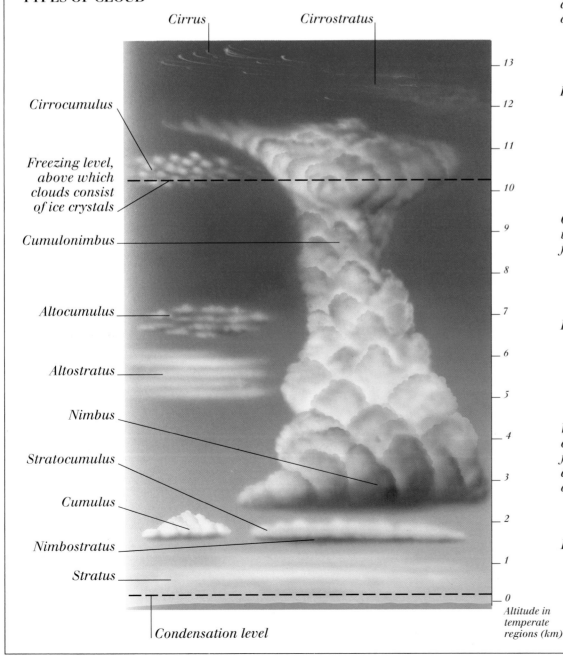

Cirrus

Cirrostratus

Cirrocumulus

Freezing level, above which clouds consist of ice crystals

Cumulonimbus

Altocumulus

Altostratus

Nimbus

Stratocumulus

Cumulus

Nimbostratus

Stratus

13
12
11
10
9
8
7
6
5
4
3
2
1
0

Altitude in temperate regions (km)

Condensation level

TYPES OF OCCLUDED FRONT

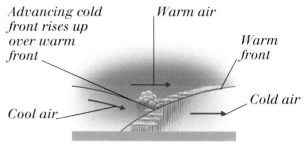

Advancing cold front rises up over warm front

Warm air

Warm front

Cool air

Cold air

WARM OCCLUSION

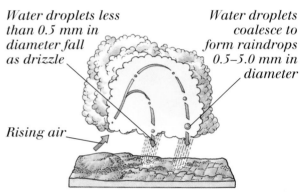

Cold air

Warm air

Warm front

Cold front undercuts warm front

Cool air

COLD OCCLUSION

FORMS OF PRECIPITATION

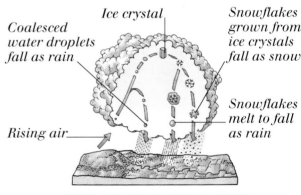

Water droplets less than 0.5 mm in diameter fall as drizzle

Water droplets coalesce to form raindrops 0.5–5.0 mm in diameter

Rising air

RAIN FROM CLOUDS NOT REACHING FREEZING LEVEL

Coalesced water droplets fall as rain

Ice crystal

Snowflakes grown from ice crystals fall as snow

Snowflakes melt to fall as rain

Rising air

RAIN AND SNOW FROM CLOUDS REACHING FREEZING LEVEL

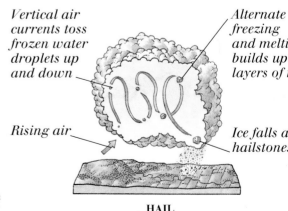

Vertical air currents toss frozen water droplets up and down

Alternate freezing and melting builds up layers of ice

Rising air

Ice falls as hailstones

HAIL

STRUCTURE OF A HURRICANE

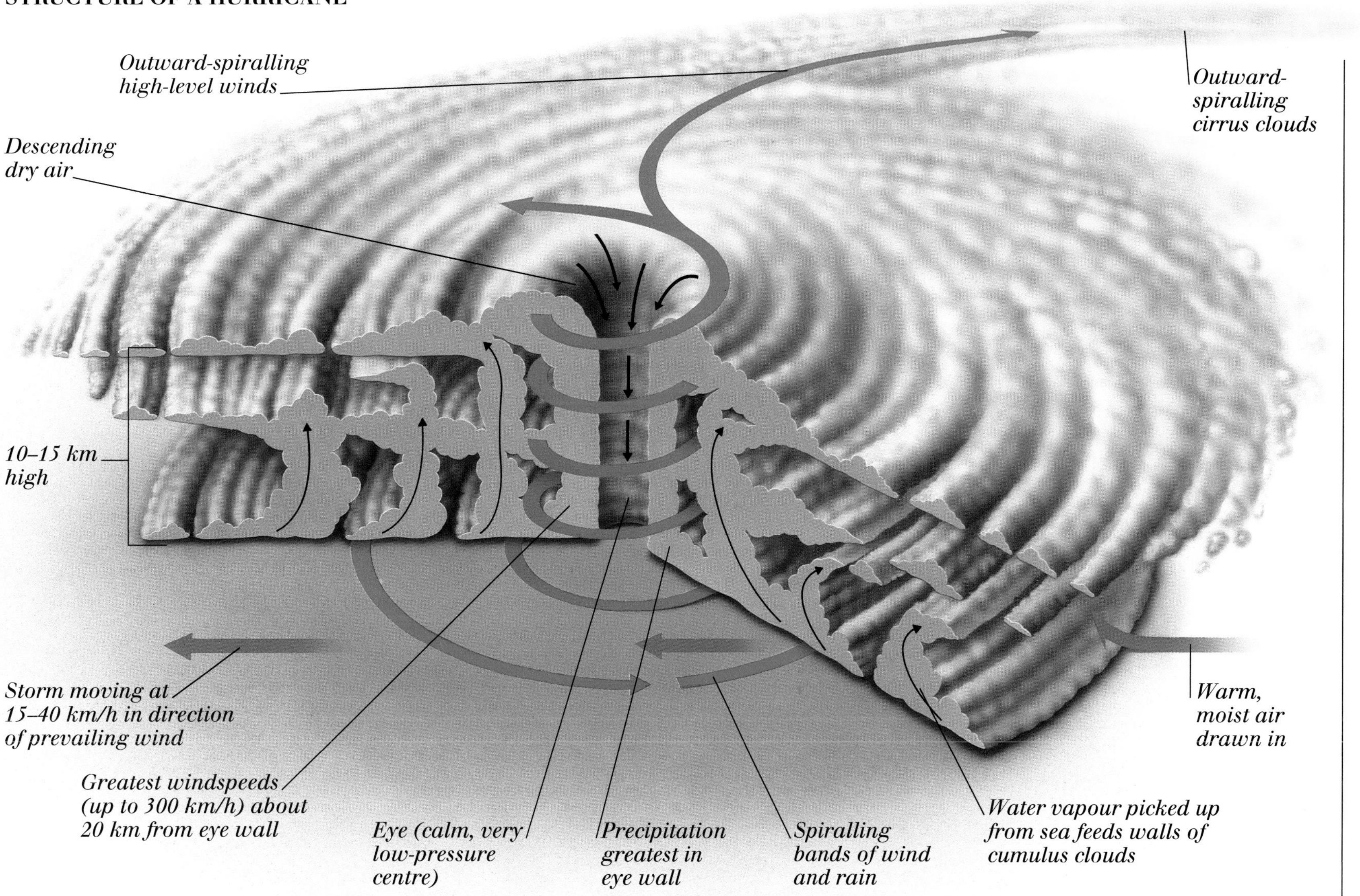

Outward-spiralling high-level winds

Descending dry air

Outward-spiralling cirrus clouds

10–15 km high

Storm moving at 15–40 km/h in direction of prevailing wind

Warm, moist air drawn in

Greatest windspeeds (up to 300 km/h) about 20 km from eye wall

Eye (calm, very low-pressure centre)

Precipitation greatest in eye wall

Spiralling bands of wind and rain

Water vapour picked up from sea feeds walls of cumulus clouds

WEATHER MAP

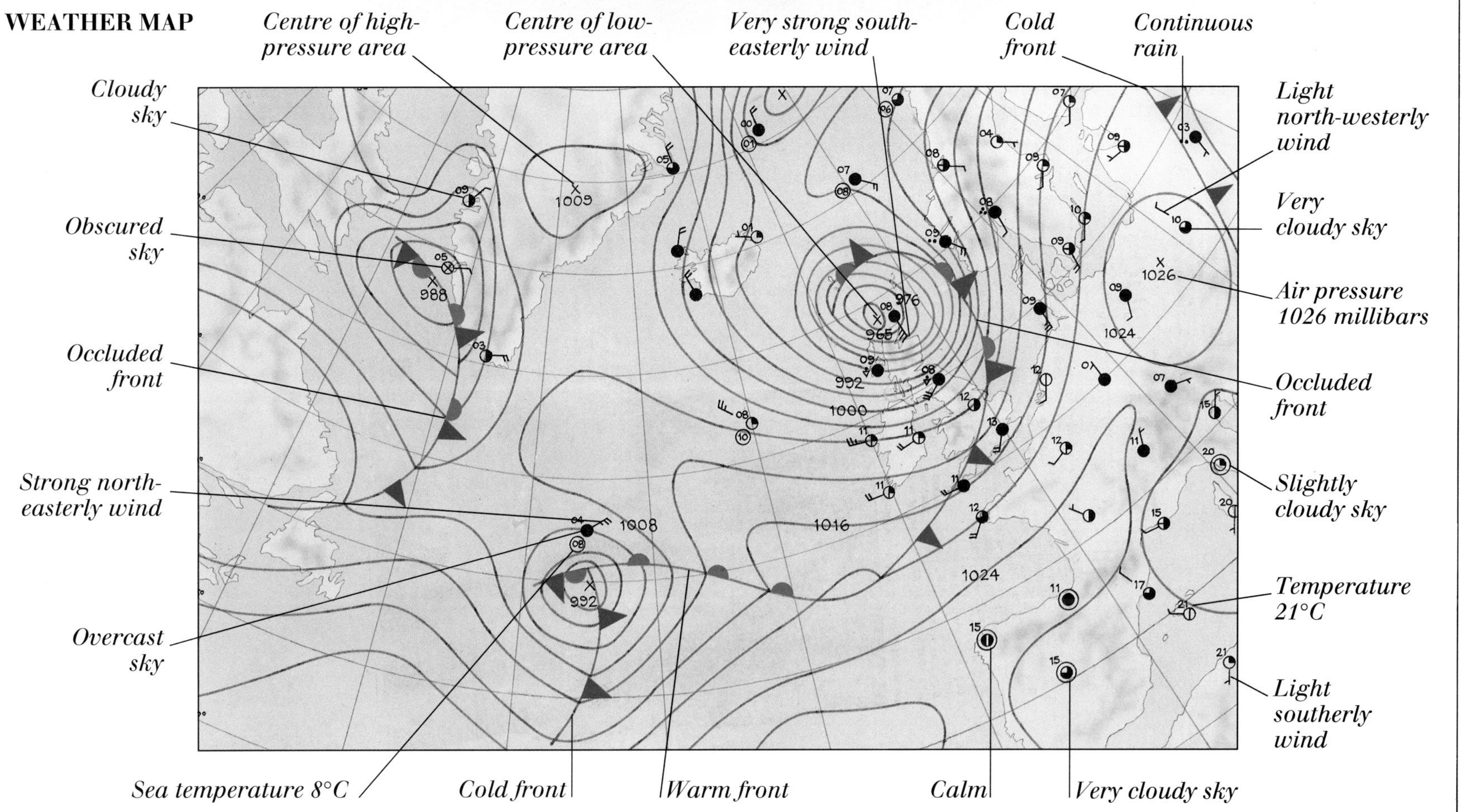

Centre of high-pressure area

Centre of low-pressure area

Very strong south-easterly wind

Cold front

Continuous rain

Cloudy sky

Light north-westerly wind

Obscured sky

Very cloudy sky

Occluded front

Air pressure 1026 millibars

Strong north-easterly wind

Occluded front

Slightly cloudy sky

Overcast sky

Temperature 21°C

Sea temperature 8°C

Cold front

Warm front

Calm

Very cloudy sky

Light southerly wind

55

Earth data

EARTH PROFILE

Average distance from Sun (km)	149,600,000
Maximum distance from Sun (km)	152,100,000
Minimum distance from Sun (km)	147,100,000
Length of year (days)	365.26
Length of day (hours)	23.93
Surface temperature range (°C)	-88.3 to 58.0
Mass (billion billion tonnes)	5,976
Volume (km^3)	1,083,230,000,000
Axial tilt (degrees)	23.5
Specific gravity (water = 1)	5.52
Polar diameter (km)	12,714
Equatorial diameter (km)	12,756
Polar circumference (km)	40,008
Equatorial circumference (km)	40,075
Total surface area (km^2)	510,000,000
Land surface area (km^2)	149,000,000
Land as % of total surface area	29.2
Water surface area (km^2)	361,000,000
Water as % of total surface area	70.8
Highest point on land (m)	8,848
Lowest point on land (m below sea level)	400
Average height of land (m)	840
Greatest ocean depth (m)	10,924
Average ocean depth (m)	3,808
Oceanic crust thickness (km)	6
Continental crust thickness (km)	40
Mantle thickness (km)	2,800
Outer core thickness (km)	2,300
Inner core diameter (km)	2,400
Approximate age of Earth (millions of years)	4,600

OCEANS AND SEAS

	Name	Area (km^2)	Average depth (m)
LARGEST AND DEEPEST	Pacific Ocean	166,229,000	4,028
	Atlantic Ocean	86,551,000	3,926
	Indian Ocean	73,422,000	3,963
	Arctic Ocean	13,223,000	1,205
	South China Sea	2,975,000	1,652
	Caribbean Sea	2,516,000	2,467
	Mediterranean Sea	2,509,000	1,429
	Bering Sea	2,261,000	1,547
	Gulf of Mexico	1,508,000	1,486
	Sea of Okhotsk	1,392,000	840
	Sea of Japan	1,013,000	1,370
	Hudson Bay	730,000	120
	East China Sea	665,000	180
	Black Sea	508,000	1,100
	Red Sea	453,000	490
	North Sea	427,000	90

	Length (km)	Deepest point	Depth (m)
DEEP SEA TRENCHES			
Mariana Trench (W. Pacific)	2,250	Challenger Deep	10,924
Tonga-Kermadec Trench (S. Pacific)	2,575	Vityaz II (Tonga)	10,800
Kuril-Kamchatka Trench (W. Pacific)	2,250	Unnamed	10,542
Philippine Trench (W. Pacific)	1,325	Galathea Deep	10,539
Solomon/New Britain Trench (S. Pacific)	640	Unnamed	8,940
Puerto Rico Trench (W. Atlantic)	800	Milwaukee Deep	8,605
Yap Trench (W. Pacific)	560	Unnamed	8,527
Japan Trench (W. Pacific)	1,600	Unnamed	8,412
South Sandwich Trench (S. Atlantic)	965	Meteor Deep	8,325

CONTINENTS

	Name	Area (km^2)	% of total surface area	% of total land area	Highest point	Height (m)	Lowest point	Below sea level (m)
	Asia	44,000,000	8.6	29.5	Mt. Everest	8,848	Dead Sea	400
	Africa	30,000,000	5.9	20.1	Kilimanjaro	5,895	Lac Assal	156
	N. America	24,000,000	4.7	16.1	Denali (Mt. McKinley)	6,194	Death Valley	86
	S. America	18,000,000	3.5	12.1	Aconcagua	6,960	Peninsular Valdez	40
	Antarctica	14,000,000	2.7	9.4	Vinson Massif	5,140	Bently Subglacial Trench	2,538
	Europe	10,000,000	2.0	6.7	El'brus	5,642	Caspian Sea	28
	Australasia	9,000,000	1.8	6.1	Mt. Wilhelm	4,884	Lake Eyre	16

ISLANDS

	Name	Area (km^2)
LARGEST	Greenland	2,175,219
	New Guinea	792,493
	Borneo	725,416
	Madagascar	587,009
	Baffin Island (Canada)	507,423
	Sumatra	427,325
	Honshu (Japan)	227,401
	Great Britain	218,065
	Victoria Island (Canada)	217,278
	Ellesmere Island (Canada)	196,225

LAKES AND INLAND SEAS

	Name	Area (km^2)
LARGEST	Caspian Sea (Asia/Europe)	370,980
	Lake Superior (N. America)	82,098
	Lake Victoria (Africa)	69,480
	Aral Sea (Asia)	64,498
	Lake Huron (N. America)	59,566
	Lake Michigan (N. America)	57,754
	Lake Tanganyika (Africa)	32,891
	Lake Baikal (Asia)	31,498
	Great Bear Lake (N. America)	31,197
	Lake Nyasa (Africa)	28,877

MOUNTAINS

	Name	Height (m)
HIGHEST	Mt. Everest (Tibet/Nepal)	8,848
	K2 (Pakistan/Tibet)	8,611
	Kangchenjunga (India/Nepal)	8,598
	Makalu (Tibet/Nepal)	8,480
	Cho Oyu (Tibet/Nepal)	8,201
	Dhaulagiri (Nepal)	8,172
	Nanga Parbat (India)	8,126
	Annapurna (Nepal)	8,078
	Gasherbrum (India)	8,068
	Xixabangma Feng (Tibet)	8,013

ACTIVE VOLCANOES

	Name	Height (m)
HIGHEST	Guallatiri (Chile)	6,060
	Lascar (Chile)	5,990
	Cotopaxi (Ecuador)	5,897
	Tupungatito (Chile)	5,640
	Ruiz (Colombia)	5,400
	Sangay (Ecuador)	5,230
	Purace (Colombia)	4,755
	Klyuchevskaya Sopka (Russia)	4,750
	Colima (Mexico)	4,268
	Galeras (Colombia)	4,266

RIVERS

	Name	Length (km)
LONGEST	River Nile (Africa)	6,695
	Amazon River (S. America)	6,437
	Yangtze River/Chang Jiang (Asia)	6,379
	Mississippi-Missouri River (N. America)	6,264
	River Ob-Irtysh (Asia)	5,411
	Yellow River/Huang He (Asia)	4,672
	River Congo/Zaire (Africa)	4,667
	River Amur (Asia)	4,416
	River Lena (Asia)	4,400
	Mackenzie-Peace River (N. America)	4,241

DESERTS

	Name	Area (km²)
LARGEST	Sahara (Africa)	8,800,000
	Gobi Desert (Asia)	1,300,000
	Australian Desert (Australasia)	1,250,000
	Arabian Desert (Asia)	850,000
	Kalahari Desert (Africa)	580,000
	Chihuahuan Desert (N. America)	370,000
	Takla Makan Desert (Asia)	320,000
	Kara Kum (Asia)	310,000
	Namib Desert (Africa)	310,000
	Thar Desert (Asia)	260,000

WATERFALLS

	Name	Height (m)
HIGHEST DROP	Angel Falls (Venezuela)	979
	Tugela Falls (South Africa)	853
	Utgaard (Norway)	800
	Mongefossen (Norway)	774
	Yosemite Falls (USA)	739
	Mardalsfossen (Norway)	655
	Cuquenan Falls (Venezuela)	610
	Sutherland Falls (New Zealand)	580
	Ribbon Falls (USA)	491
	Gavarnie (France)	422

	Name	Volume (m³/sec)
GREATEST VOLUME	Boyoma Falls (Zaire)	17,000
	Guaira Falls (Brazil/Paraguay)	13,000
	Khone Falls (Laos)	11,500
	Niagara Falls (Canada/USA)	6,000
	Paulo Afonso Falls (Brazil)	2,800
	Urubupunga Falls (Brazil)	2,700
	Cataras del Iguazu Falls (Brazil/Paraguay)	1,700
	Patos-Maribondo Falls (Brazil)	1,500
	Victoria Falls (Zimbabwe)	1,100
	Churchill Falls (Canada)	1,000

CAVES

	Name	Depth (m)
DEEPEST	Reseau Jean Bernard (France)	1,602
	Shakta Pantjukhina (Georgia)	1,508
	Lamrechtsofen (Austria)	1,485
	Sistema del Trave (Spain)	1,441
	Boj Bulok (Uzbekistan)	1,415

	Name	Length (km)
LONGEST SYSTEMS	Mammoth Cave System (USA)	560
	Optimisticheskaya (Ukraine)	183
	Hölloch (Switzerland)	137
	Jewel Cave (USA)	127
	Ozernaya (Ukraine)	107

GLACIERS

	Name	Length (km)
LONGEST	Lambert-Fisher Ice Passage (Antarctica)	515
	Novaya Zemlya (Russia)	418
	Arctic Institute Ice Passage (Antarctica)	362
	Nimrod-Lennox-King Ice Passage (Antarctica)	289
	Denman Glacier (Antarctica)	241
	Beardmore Glacier (Antarctica)	225
	Recovery Glacier (Antarctica)	225
	Petermanns Gletscher (Greenland)	200
	Unnamed glacier (Antarctica)	193
	Slessor Glacier (Antarctica)	185

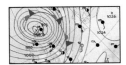

WEATHER

Records

Highest recorded temperature:
  58°C at Al' Aziziyah, Libya, 13 September 1922.
Lowest recorded temperature:
  -88.3°C at Vostok, Antarctica, 24 August 1960.
Greatest average yearly rainfall:
  11,455 mm at Mt. Wai'ale'ale, Hawaii.
Greatest recorded rainfall in any one year:
  26,461 mm at Cherrapunji, India, in 1860–61.
Windiest place:
  Commonwealth Bay, Antarctica, where several
  320 km/h winds occur each year.
Highest recorded windspeed:
  371 km/h on Mt. Washington, USA, in 1934.

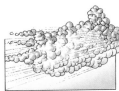

WINDSPEED

	No.	Description	Speed (km/h)	Characteristics
BEAUFORT SCALE	0	Calm	Below 1	Smoke rises vertically.
	1	Light air	1–5	Smoke blown by wind.
	2	Light breeze	6–12	Leaves rustle.
	3	Gentle breeze	13–20	Extends a light flag.
	4	Moderate breeze	21–29	Raises dust and loose paper.
	5	Fresh breeze	30–39	Small trees begin to sway.
	6	Strong breeze	40–50	Large branches in motion.
	7	Near gale	51–61	Whole trees in motion.
	8	Gale	62–74	Twigs broken off trees.
	9	Strong gale	75–87	Structural damage occurs.
	10	Storm	88–102	Trees uprooted.
	11	Violent storm	103–120	Widespread damage.
	12–17	Hurricane	Over 120	Extremely violent.

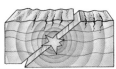

EARTHQUAKES

	Magnitude	Probable effects
RICHTER SCALE	1	Detectable only by instruments.
	2–2.5	Barely detectable even near epicentre.
	4–5	Detectable within 32 km of epicentre; may cause slight damage.
	6	Moderately destructive.
	7	A major earthquake.
	8–9	A very destructive earthquake.

CHEMICAL ELEMENTS

●	Ac	Actinium	● Mn	Manganese
●	Ag	Silver	● Mo	Molybdenum
○	Al	Aluminium	○ N	Nitrogen
●	Am	Americium	● Na	Sodium
○	Ar	Argon	● Nb	Niobium
○	As	Arsenic	● Nd	Neodymium
○	At	Astatine	○ Ne	Neon
●	Au	Gold	● Ni	Nickel
○	B	Boron	● No	Nobelium
●	Ba	Barium	● Np	Neptunium
●	Be	Beryllium	○ O	Oxygen
○	Bi	Bismuth	● Os	Osmium
●	Bk	Berkelium	○ P	Phosphorus
○	Br	Bromine	● Pa	Protactinium
○	C	Carbon	○ Pb	Lead
●	Ca	Calcium	● Pd	Palladium
●	Cd	Cadmium	● Pm	Promethium
●	Ce	Cerium	○ Po	Polonium
●	Cf	Californium	● Pr	Praseodymium
○	Cl	Chlorine	● Pt	Platinum
●	Cm	Curium	● Pu	Plutonium
●	Co	Cobalt	● Ra	Radium
●	Cr	Chromium	● Rb	Rubidium
●	Cs	Caesium	● Re	Rhenium
●	Cu	Copper	● Rf-Ku	Rutherfordium-Kurchatovium
●	Dy	Dysprosium		
●	Er	Erbium	● Rh	Rhodium
●	Es	Einsteinium	○ Rn	Radon
●	Eu	Europium	● Ru	Ruthenium
○	F	Fluorine	○ S	Sulphur
●	Fe	Iron	○ Sb	Antimony
●	Fm	Fermium	● Sc	Scandium
●	Fr	Francium	○ Se	Selenium
○	Ga	Gallium	○ Si	Silicon
●	Gd	Gadolinium	● Sm	Samarium
○	Ge	Germanium	○ Sn	Tin
●	H	Hydrogen	● Sr	Strontium
●	Ha	Hahnium	● Ta	Tantalum
●	He	Helium	● Tb	Terbium
●	Hf	Hafnium	● Tc	Technetium
●	Hg	Mercury	○ Te	Tellurium
●	Ho	Holmium	● Th	Thorium
○	I	Iodine	● Ti	Titanium
○	In	Indium	● Tl	Thallium
●	Ir	Iridium	● Tm	Thulium
●	K	Potassium	● U	Uranium
●	Kr	Krypton	● V	Vanadium
●	La	Lanthanum	● W	Tungsten
●	Li	Lithium	○ Xe	Xenon
●	Lr	Lawrencium	● Y	Yttrium
●	Lu	Lutetium	● Yb	Ytterbium
●	Md	Mendelevium	● Zn	Zinc
●	Mg	Magnesium	● Zr	Zirconium

●	Alkaline earth metals	○	Lanthanide series
●	Alkali metals	○	Actinide series
○	Other metals	○	Non-metals
●	Transition metals	○	Noble gases

● Hydrogen is a gas with unique properties and is therefore usually placed in a group by itself.

Glossary

AQUIFER: A layer of water-saturated permeable rock lying on a layer of impermeable rock. It can be a source of water for wells and springs.

ARTESIAN BASIN: An aquifer in which water is held under pressure between two layers of impermeable rock. (See also Aquifer.)

ASTHENOSPHERE: A partly molten layer of the Earth's mantle below the lithosphere. (See also Lithosphere; Mantle.)

ATMOSPHERE: The layer of gases surrounding the Earth, consisting of (from ground-level upwards) the troposphere, stratosphere, mesosphere, thermosphere, and exosphere.

BATHOLITH: A large, domed, igneous intrusion composed of granitic rock.

BED: A layer or stratum of rock (usually sedimentary). A **competent bed** is one liable to break under stress. An **incompetent bed** is one liable to bend or flow under stress.

CALDERA: A basin-shaped volcanic depression, typically resulting from an eruption and/or collapse of a volcano.

CLEAVAGE: The tendency of a mineral to break along well-defined planes of weakness.

CLIMATE: The average weather conditions for a region over a long period of time. (See also Weather.)

CONTINENTAL DRIFT: The theory that today's continents were formed by the break-up of prehistoric supercontinents that have slowly drifted to their present positions. (See also Plate tectonics.)

CORE: The central portion of the Earth, made up of a solid inner core and a molten outer core.

CORIOLIS FORCE: A force that results from the Earth's rotation. It deflects winds and water to the right in the Northern Hemisphere and to the left in the Southern Hemisphere.

CRUST: The outer layer of the Earth lying above the mantle. There are two main types: continental and oceanic crust.

CRYSTAL: A geometric form of a mineral, with naturally formed plane faces that reflect the arrangement of its constituent atoms.

DESERT: An arid region where precipitation is generally less than 250 mm per year.

EARTHQUAKE: Shock waves, sometimes causing violent tremors at the Earth's surface, caused in most cases by sudden crustal displacement along a fault. (See also Epicentre; Focus.)

ELEMENT: A substance that cannot be broken down by chemical means into simpler substances.

EON: A division of geological time that can be subdivided into eras (see Era).

EPICENTRE: The point on the Earth's surface directly above the focus of an earthquake. (See also Earthquake; Focus.)

EPOCH: A division of geological time that is a subdivision of a period (see Period).

ERA: A division of geological time that is a subdivision of an eon and which can be subdivided into a period. (See also Eon; Period.)

EROSION: The wearing away and removal of exposed land by water, wind, and/or ice. (See also Weathering.)

EXOSPHERE: The outermost layer of the atmosphere (see Atmosphere).

FAULT: A fracture in a rock along which there may be displacement of one side relative to the other.

FOCUS: The point underground at which an earthquake originates. (See also Earthquake; Epicentre.)

FOLD: A buckle or bend in a rock layer due to horizontal pressure in the Earth's crust. An **anticline** is an arch-shaped fold. A **syncline** is a trough-shaped fold.

FOSSIL: The remains, traces, or impressions of plants and animals that have been preserved in rock.

FRACTURE: The tendency of a mineral or rock to break in an irregular way.

FRONT: The boundary between two air masses. At a **warm front**, warm air rises up over cold air; at a **cold front**, cold air pushes under warm air.

GLACIER: A large mass of ice that forms on land and moves slowly downhill under its own weight.

GREENHOUSE EFFECT: The process in which radiation from the Sun passes through the atmosphere, is reflected and re-radiated from the Earth's surface, and is then trapped by atmospheric gases. The build-up of "greenhouse gases", such as carbon dioxide, has increased the effect, leading to global warming.

GROUNDMASS: The finer-grained material of a rock in which larger crystals or pebbles are embedded. **Matrix** is an alternative term for groundmass.

GROUNDWATER: Water accumulated beneath the Earth's surface.

GUTENBERG DISCONTINUITY: The boundary between the mantle and the outer core.

GYRE: The circular rotation of the waters of the major oceans and seas, driven by winds and the Coriolis force. (See also Coriolis force.)

HABIT: The typical form taken by an aggregate of a mineral's crystals.

IGNEOUS ROCK: A rock that is formed from solidified magma or lava. **Intrusive igneous rocks** are formed underground; **extrusive igneous rocks** are formed on the surface.

LAVA: Molten magma expelled on to the Earth's surface through volcanoes or fissures. The two most common forms in which lava solidifies are known as **aa** (irregular jagged blocks), and **pahoehoe** (rope-like strands).

LITHIFICATION: The formation of rock from unconsolidated sediment by the processes of compression and cementation. (See also Sedimentary rock.)

LITHOSPHERE: The Earth's crust and the topmost layer of the mantle.

LONGSHORE DRIFT: Movement of sand and small rocks along the seashore, driven by the action of waves.

MAGMA: Molten rock originating in the Earth's mantle and crust.

MANTLE: The layer of the Earth between the outer core and the crust.

MESOSPHERE: The layer of the atmosphere above the stratosphere and below the thermosphere. (See also Atmosphere.)

METAMORPHIC ROCK: A rock that is formed from previously existing rocks that have been subjected to intense heat and/or pressure, to the extent that their chemical composition has been altered.

MINERAL: A naturally occurring substance that has a characteristic chemical composition and specific physical properties.

MOHOROVICIC DISCONTINUITY: The boundary between the crust and mantle.

MOHS SCALE: A scale by which the relative hardness of minerals can be measured.

OROGENESIS: The term used to describe the processes involved in mountain building.

PERIOD: A division of geological time that is a subdivision of an era and which can be subdivided into an epoch. (See also Epoch; Era.)

PLATE TECTONICS: The theory that the Earth's lithosphere consists of several semi-rigid plates that move relative to each other.

PRECIPITATION: All forms of water particles that fall from clouds, including rain, hail, sleet, and snow.

PYROCLAST: A rock formed from the debris of an explosive volcanic eruption.

ROCK: An aggregate of minerals. Rocks are divided into three main groups: igneous, metamorphic, and sedimentary (see Igneous rock; Metamorphic rock; Sedimentary rock).

ROCK CYCLE: The continuous cycle through which old rocks are transformed into new ones.

SEA-FLOOR SPREADING: The process by which new sea-floor crust is created at ridges in mid-ocean where two adjacent plates move away from each other. (See also Plate tectonics.)

SEDIMENTARY ROCK: A rock formed by the lithification of sediment. (See also Lithification.)

SPRING: A flow of groundwater that emerges naturally on the Earth's surface.

STRATOSPHERE: The layer of the atmosphere above the troposphere and below the mesosphere. (See also Atmosphere.)

STRATUM: A layer or bed of rock. (See also Bed.)

STREAK: The colour that a powdered mineral makes when rubbed across an unglazed tile.

SUBDUCTION ZONE: An area where one plate is forced under another. (See also Plate tectonics.)

THERMOSPHERE: The highest layer of the atmosphere. (See also Atmosphere.)

TIDE: The regular rise and fall of the ocean surface resulting principally from the gravitational forces between the Earth, Moon, and Sun.

TRAP: A folded or faulted layer of impermeable rock beneath which oil and gas may accumulate.

TRENCH: A long, narrow valley on the ocean floor found along a subduction zone. (See also Subduction zone.)

TROPOSPHERE: The lowest layer of the atmosphere. (See also Atmosphere.)

UNCONFORMITY: A major break in a sequence of rock strata that represents a period when no new sediments were being laid down and/or when earlier sedimentary layers were eroded away.

VOLCANO: A vent or fissure in the Earth's crust through which molten magma and hot gases escape. Most volcanoes occur along plate boundaries.

WATER CYCLE: The processes by which water is circulated between land, the oceans, and the atmosphere. An alternative name is the **hydrologic cycle**.

WATER TABLE: The level up to which the ground is permanently saturated.

WEATHER: The atmospheric conditions at a particular time and place. (See also Climate.)

WEATHERING: The breaking down of rocks when they are exposed on the Earth's surface by physical (mechanical) or chemical means. (See also Erosion.)

Index

Acknowledgments

Dorling Kindersley would like to thank:
Dr. John Nudds, The Manchester Museum, Manchester; Dr. Alan Wooley and Dr. Andrew Clark, The Natural History Museum, London; Graham Bartlett, National Meteorological Library and Archive, Bracknell; Tony Drake, BP Exploration, Uxbridge; Jane Davies, Royal Society of Chemistry, Cambridge; Dr. Tony Waltham, Nottingham Trent University, Nottingham; Staff at the Smithsonian Institute, Washington; Staff at the United States Geological Survey, Washington; Staff at the National Geographic Society, Washington; Staff at Edward Lawrence Associates (Export Ltd.), Midhurst; John Farndon; David Lambert

Picture credits:
BP Exploration 51c; Bruce Coleman Ltd/Andy Price 18tl; Robert Harding jacket, 16tl; Hutchison Picture Library 14cl; Nature Photographers/ Paul Sterry 38tl; SPL/ Earth Satellite Corporation 40cl, 45br; Simon Fraser 20tl; NASA 43tr, 52tl; David Parker 17bl; Tom Van Sant 6tl, 8-9c, 19tr, 33tl, 48-49c; Floor of the Oceans, by Bruce C. Heezen and Marie Tharp 1975. © Marie Tharp 1980. Reproduced by permission of Marie Tharp, 1 Washington Ave, South Nyack, NY 10960, USA 13tr; G. Steenmans 44tl; Tony Stone Worldwide 32tl; Zefa/Janicek jacket, 28tl

(t=top, b=bottom, l=left, r=right, c=centre)

Picture research:
Christine Rista, Catherine O'Rourke, Anna Lord

Additional editorial assistance:
Emily Hill, Cathy Rubinstein

Additional design assistance:
Sue Knight

Index:
Kay Wright